THE LAZY B

Fast Eddy

ISBN-13: 978-1725695399
ISBN-10:1725695391

DEDICATION

Dedicated to my Dad, Clifford Sweeney, who gave me my start in life, and at Boeing. I'll always miss you Dad, and so will Boeing.

Also dedicated...to all the millions of devoted Boeing men and women who helped us win wars, and rule the skies.

And to the members of the International Association of Machinists and Aerospace Workers, District 751, who fought and sacrificed on the picket lines, to earn us decent pay and benefits.

Finally, dedicated to the Boeing Company, who put bread and butter on my table, gave me a wealth of experiences, and lots of stories to write about.

CONTENTS

BEFORE THIS FLIGHT TAKES OFF

Boeing was a universe unto itself. There were the "Black Holes" where those who dwelt were sworn to secrecy. There were novas, where incredible new technologies came to light. Some of the planets orbiting the Boeing star, were anything but lazy. Others within that "Milky Way", indeed were "milked", for all the gravy they had to offer.

I spent many moons in my own star-ship exploring this universe. From deep in the pits of a hot heat treat tank, scraping solidified salt off the walls, to hovering high over the Boeing world in an overhead crane, I lived and experienced both the Lazy B, and the Busy B for 37 years. And like the images from the Hubble telescope, the world of Boeing was a colorful, fascinating, place to be.

With an infinite number of people, jobs, and experiences, other people's journeys may be have been far different from my own. The "Lazy B" was commonly used referring to the whole galaxy of the Boeing culture. It's just a "tongue in cheek" nickname, not necessarily descriptive of any particular organization, job, or group of employees within the company.

Boeing has been one of the most successful American companies of all time. Mostly, due to the ingenuity and hard work of the thousands, maybe even millions of dedicated workers who have entered it's gates. Almost everyone who worked there, took a great deal of pride in this success.

Much has changed since I began as a baby faced 18 year old kid. When I retired as a prune faced, 60 year old man, the Boeing I left, had little in common with the company that I had started with, in the previous century.

But, I have no regrets about the time I spent in the golden age of the Lazy B. Boeing was good to me, and I tried to be good to it too.

I left a lot of sweat, a little bit of blood, and maybe even a couple of tears on those factory floors. The grinding of milling machines, the pounding of riveters, and the laughter of friends, still rings in my ears.

In this book, I try to give an honest account of my experiences. I'm not trying to embarrass, indict or crucify anyone. Just "telling it like it was". To protect the innocent (and the guilty), I just use first names, perhaps adding the initial of a surname, here and there.

And with some people, I change their names entirely. But I will tell you when I do so. I met a lot of great people there, and I like to brag about their attributes. I met a few whose motives were questionable. In the interest of truth and justice, I describe some of their capers in an anonymous manner.

I look back on my Boeing career fondly. I had a pretty good time making some pretty decent money. It's lost some of the spirit and the magic of the "good old days" But I think Boeing is still one of the best companies to work for.

My long odyssey in the Boeing universe, was not just a job. It was truly, my adventure in aviation. And in life.

1

BLUE BADGES

Back in the days when the Chevys ruled the roads, and the 747s ruled the skies, American manufacturing owned the globe. American men and women with sleepy eyes, wearing greasy coveralls, turned the cranks that made the world go round.

A "Made in the USA" inscription, meant quality and pride in workmanship. Depicting a confident, certain, almost arrogant, superiority in manufacturing.

The "Made in Japan" label, signified junk, cheap, and disposable. The American flag waved majestically, high and proud. Our businesses were the envy of the world. Uncle Sam walked with a strut, and a smirk.

America's allies, were scrawny little guys who hid behind their big, bad buddy. Their "would be" bullies, knew better than to mess with us. Our enemies cowered, knowing that we could clean their clocks, whether dirty or not. The USA was like their symbol, the Eagle. Imposing and fierce, with big talons, and big talents.

Our coveralls were grubby and our eyes tired, because we were expected to keep our products sitting up high on their pedestals, brightly polished. No matter how many hours it took, or how hard we had to work.

1

But companies like Boeing, made it worth our while. Paying us good money to buy those Chevys, fly in those 747s, and to live in those nice, middle class homes. The union would square off against management every few years, to guarantee that our backs were scratched.

Strong coffee flowed like rivers from our thermoses. And cigarette smoke swirled inside the factories. Just like the smokestacks that blew outside them. As the mechanics sweated, and cussed their way through another workday, the smell of perspiration, tobacco, and noxious chemicals reeked inside of the shops.

Screeches, clunks, and grinds shook the walls, as the welders, and the cutting torches maintained the inside temperatures, like Death Valley on an exceptionally hot, desert day.

Clutter was everywhere. Rope, pallets, tools, parts, and hardware littered the walkways. But the upside, was that whatever you needed was never more than a couple yards away from where you stood. Serious looking clodhoppers, with steel toes, danced around the shambles. Never tripping over the disarray. It was a well practiced, and oiled dance routine on most days.

When a big shot was going to be strolling through the shop, all productive work would come to a grinding halt, The disarray would be swept away, and valuable tools and parts would be "shit-canned", to pretty up the factory for their visit. It sometimes took hours to prepare for these quick five minute walk throughs by a VIP.

We called these mirages, "Dog and Pony Shows". And by the time they had started, overtime lists were being made to catch up for the lost time.

If I had been a big shot, I would have asked my management hosts, "Don't you guys ever DO anything around here?" I knew what a shop that was producing goods was supposed to look like. Seemingly, these executives, didn't have a clue.

The factory would be my world for many years. A couple of weeks after I grabbed my high school diploma and tossed my graduation cap, my plans for a little sabbatical from the daily grind, were changed by my Dad's ultimatum.

"Okay, so you're out of school. What are you going to do now....?" Dad asked, hands on hips, as I lounged on the couch, enjoying a cold coke in front of the TV. .

"Well, I thought I'd take the summer off... Just have a little fun, you know...And take my time to decide what to do next", I replied, with my eyes fixed on a rerun of Gilligan's Island.

Shucks, it was a big decision. I saw no need to make any hasty choices, that I might soon regret.

Dad stepped in front of the screen.

"Listen, I talked to my buddy in personnel. If you want my help getting in the door at Boeing, you'll show up for work next week in Renton. If not, then you're on your own"

The weather started getting rough. My tiny ship was tossed.

I thought it over, for a good ten seconds. They paid $4.33 an hour for starters in this $1.60 an hour era. With big raises every 3 months on the Learner Progression Program. Plus, unbelievable benefits. Hmmm...

"Well?" Dad grilled me impatiently.

I glanced out the window, watching my summer dreams of slacking, evaporating in the bright June sunshine.

"Yeah...okay. Thanks Dad."

Yeah, GEE THANKS. I'd been hitting it hard for the last 13 years. When does a guy get a little break? This working thing, could last for a good 30 or 40 years, easily. My happy little boat, which had been bobbing around in the lazy harbor waters of relaxation, just sank.

The Minnow had been lost.

But still, for an 18 year old kid, getting on at Boeing was like a guy in a rock band, starting out by playing the Coliseum. For blue collar workers, landing a job at Boeing, was hitting the big time.

I guess it still occurs to some degree. Today, they call it "networking". But in the mid 70s, nepotism, was the best thing to have on your resume.

It was often, "who you knew", more than "what you knew". The grapevine, was the best way to climb up the company ladder. You didn't HAVE to know someone to get hired. But, it sure didn't hurt your chances. In the "good old boy" system, the only qualifications that you really needed, was to be, "Cliff's son".

Boeing was a family affair. If your Dad worked there, then it was likely you would too. Many times, his Dad had worked there before him. And chances were, your kids would eventually work there too. For generations, the bacon we brought home, came in a Boeing package.

The interview was merely a formality. It had been a done deal as soon as your Dad, acting as your agent, had stepped into the personnel manager's office. Boeing's offices were crowded with Godfathers.

"I've come to ask for a favor" After his request was granted, it was certain that favor would have to be returned someday. In the dirty world of sooty factories, and mahogany offices, it was a grime syndicate. With rules of its own.

On the night before my first day at Boeing, my brother in law's father, "Pene" was visiting from Michigan. He was nearing the end of his road of working at Pontiac, as I was first turning my key to drive into Boeing for the first time.

"You got hired at Boeing?" he beamed. "Great! What are you going to be doing?"

"I'm starting as a maintenance painter...Summer help" I bragged.

"Maintenance?" he exclaimed with envy. "The first thing you need to do, is to find a place to HIDE"

I laughed.

No, I thought, I won't need a hiding place. I'm going to work hard, and be the best darn maintenance painter that Boeing ever had! As a veteran of mowing lawns, paper routes, and helping my Uncle Boyd paint houses, I was no stranger to hard work. I intended to become the "rookie of the year"

As it turns out, Pene wasn't that far off.

Proudly flashing my badge, with my young face smiling under it's blue bar and the Boeing logo, I strutted into my work station, a whole five minutes early. Swinging my metal working man's lunch-pail, in my eager hands.

"Hi, I'm Dick" the lead-man said. I would meet a lot of Dicks throughout my career at Boeing.

"Hi, I'm Ed. What do you want me to do first, Dick...?" I asked dutifully.

"I want you to slow down, and take it easy" Dick chuckled.

"Well, I'm all ready to go, Dick...."

"Well I'm NOT", Dick answered, starting up a pot of coffee.

"You see that blue bar on your badge, Ed?"

I nodded.

5

"That means you're in Maintenance. We're nomads. We roam around the plant. We don't have a regular work station. We're not production workers, with a boss breathing down our backs every minute. We PACE ourselves around here. Relax, Ed."

It was uncomfortable. I was worried about getting "canned" even before I saw my first payday. Making this kind of money, I believed I ought to be busy every minute.

But my boss, "Frosty", had told me to do whatever Dick said to do. So, I tried to settle down. Changing from pacing nervously in the maintenance shed, to just doing some light fidgeting in place.

Dick introduced me to the guys. His buddy and right hand man, was Glen. They were both down home, Southern country boys with Tennessee accents. Wearing hospitable smiles, they both had those, "sipping ice tea on the front porch" laid back attitudes.

Dick's voice sounded like the football announcer, Don Meredith. "Looks like another 'time out'", he would frequently announce, in not so many words. Glen and Dick were old guys. They must have been somewhere in their mid 30s.

The rest of the crew was young.

Bob was an easy going kid, who had also just graduated from high school. Bob came from Hazen, right in Renton Boeing's back yard. Bob and I hit it off right away. Bob's friend Rick, was a nerdy college kid. Rick had also come from Hazen, a year before Bob.

John, was a snooty "frat brat", from the University of Washington. His Dad was some big Boeing company executive. John figured that his silver spoon let him do pretty much anything he wanted to. Or not do, whatever he didn't want to do. He was probably right about the magical powers of that spoon.

Some of the other kids had already been on the crew for nearly a week, on the day that I started. So, they had already learned to relax,

THE LAZY "b"

and appreciate the perks of the blue bar badge. Before long, blue would become my favorite color.

After a long pre-work break of working man trash talk, painter's banter, and southern hospitality ..."Y'all need to warm that there coffee cup, Ed...", we were finally ready to roll. To the gas pumps that is.

Taking the "scenic route" in the old Dodge panel truck, Dick milked couple of miles of sightseeing around the plant before arriving at the gas pumps. The pumps were only a half a block from the maintenance shack where we had started. By now, the tank really was getting dry.

Glen leaped to fill the tank, while Dick fiddled with the radio. The dial landed on Country Western. Hearing the twang, the young guys in the back of the panel truck rolled their eyes. We'd been listening to KJR's top 40 hits during the ride, and weren't pleased to have the Rolling Stones interrupted, by Conway Twitty.

One of Glen's buddies pulled up on a bicycle, and they had a long, detailed conversation, before any gasoline stared flowing. There was no such thing as a quick fill up, when you had a blue badge.

Meanwhile, Dick and the boys kept up a steady flow of chatter. Raising their voices, over the rambling morning DJ, at Country KAYO.

By the time we arrived at the job site, it was only about a half an hour before our first OFFICIAL break. It was way too close to break time to get started on anything, according to Dick.

So, the crew killed time for the next 40 minutes. I peered around, looking for the boss coming up to fire us all. Frosty never showed.

Right on the dot, when our official ten minute break ended, Dick suggested, "Well gentlemen, shall we...?"

7

As the rest of the guys barreled out of the panel truck, Glen looked at Dick sideways.

"Getting kinda pushy there, aren't ya buddy", his eyes seemed to say. Glen liked to take things slow and easy. Dick smiled, and shrugged his shoulders at his friend.

Almost apologetically, Dick turned to Rick and Bob and asked, "Hey, would you boys mind getting them paint cans out of the back?"

He knew better than to ask John. The frat boy had shown Dick during the last week, that all this painting stuff was far beneath him. He constantly reminded everyone, that his Dad was an executive, up on "Mahogany Row"

John watched Bob, Rick, and I drag the five gallon cans of paint out of the van, and place them next to a ragged rope that was dangling down from the roof far above.

As expected, John stationed himself by the buckets, and tied the wire bail of the first can to the rope. It was big of him, to help us out a little. Even doing the easiest job of all.

"Just don't get used to it" he smirked. John was the crew's poster boy, for privilege and entitlement.

One at a time, the rest of the crew scaled the 60 foot ladder to the roof of the 4-20 building. The climb didn't faze the other kids. But Dick and Glen, the old guys, needed a little breather after ascending up that grueling climb. As the fat kid, so did I.

I was only into the industrial world for a couple hours. But by now, I was realizing that for blue badges like us, every small achievement earned us a big, long break.

So we took it easy for a few minutes. Up high on the hot tar mopped roof, I had a bird's eye view of the whole Renton plant, and its surrounding area.

Catching my breath, I gazed across all of Renton. To the west, I could see the Cedar River dumping it's pure, mountain melted snow water into Lake Washington, mixed with all of the factory's colorful industrial waste.

Looking to the north, I saw the ramp where the newly born Boeing Hydrofoils would make their virgin plunges into the lake. Across the water, there was lush Mercer Island, as green as the money of the rich folks who lived there.

To the south, the smokestacks from Paccar were puffing little clouds of smoke into the blues skies. Interstate 405, looked like a slot car race track. The cars looked tiny, whizzing by the "S" curves, past downtown Renton.

Standing on this rooftop, I felt on top of the world. Just out of High School, making top money, in an easy, laid back, work environment. I had climbed to the peak of Blue Collar Mountain. and planted my flag. So far, this Boeing thing wasn't bad at all.

But the thud of the first five gallon can of paint pounding the black tar floor, aroused me from my daydream.

"Oh, I'm supposed to be working", I reminded myself, dashing over to the landing, to lend a hand.

Rick was dropping the rope back down for the second load of paint, while Bob was picking up the first can to pack it over to our nearby starting point.

"Here, I'll get that" I offered to Bob.

"That's alright, I've got it", Bob answered with a friendly smile.

"You can lift the next one..." Rick said, rubbing his sore biceps. Rick was always anxious to divvy up the workload, evenly. At the UW, he was probably studying to be an accountant.

John tied on the second can. I had to lean out over the edge a bit to keep the heavy can from bashing into the siding of the building, like a wrecking ball.

The cans started out fairly heavy. By the time we pulled them up 60 feet, they weighed a ton. My arms felt like I'd pulled a prize salmon up from the depths of Lake Washington. So, we took turns lifting the cans, and packing them over to the nearby job site.

There were no safety railings at the edge of the roof. If a guy wasn't careful, he could have easily followed the same path down that the cans came up. One wrong move, and we would be a smear on the pavement. It made me a little nervous. But, I guessed that was why they paid us the big bucks.

The 4-20 building's roof had a "saw-tooth" design. Ramps of tarred roof dropped off to walls of metal siding, dotted with windows.

This let the natural light filter into the building, sparing the electric lights inside the factory. And vented off some of the heat in the summertime. Our job, was going to be to repaint the worn and peeling paint, on that siding.

It was pretty close to 10 am by this time, and lunch would be at 11.

With lunch being so close, Dick decided there wasn't much sense in us getting started on the painting, until after lunch. We kids, joined Dick and Glen, sitting on paint cans in the shade of the siding walls. John, was nowhere to be seen.

Not five minutes into our fourth break before lunch time, I heard the sound of steel toed wing tips shoes, over my shoulder. Turning my head, I was shocked to see our supervisor, Frosty, standing with his hands on his hips, dressed in his supervisor monkey suit. All the bosses wore suits and ties back then.

I stood up. Oh man, we're in trouble now, I figured. I braced myself for a scolding, and maybe even a walk out the gate. I just about peed my Fruit of the Looms, waiting to be given a "pink slip" instead....

"Hey boss" Dick smiled. "Take a load off...." He motioned to an empty 5 gallon paint can seat. Frosty looked at his watch.

"Break time, is it?"

"We worked through our break, Chief", Dick claimed

"Okay. Well, how goes the battle?" Frosty asked, scanning his eyes up and down the wall. Peeling and faded, it looked like it was hungry for a paint job.

Glen, didn't take kindly to Frosty's gentle accusations of us goldbricking.

"Did you think the tooth fairy brought all these cans of paint up here? We've been hard at it!"

I couldn't believe Glen could talk to our "Superior" that way. My own Uncle would have canned me if I'd sassed him like that, while I was painting for him. But this was Boeing. As I would soon learn, a little bit of backtalk, was light years away from being punishable "insubordination", around here.

The boss looked at his clipboard. There was a thick stack of "to do", Puget Sound Maintenance work orders under it's clip. He looked worried.

"Are you boys interested in working ten hour days this week?" he asked, peering around to each of our faces.

The new guys eyes lit up like cash registers, as we calculated how fat this overtime would make our checks on payday. We all smiled, and nodded our eager acceptance of the overtime offer.

"Whatever..." Glen said indifferently, lighting up a Camel.

"If it'll make you smile, boss..." Dick said with a smile.

"Okay, how about the weekend?" Frosty asked as he scribbled on his sheet.

The youngsters eyes grew bigger, as we scratched our previous tally of our paychecks in our heads, and penciled in the inflated figures. "Sure", we all said.

Dick and Glen just rolled their eyes. Offers of extra money were so common, that they no longer excited these maintenance veterans. They were both well accustomed to selling out their free time, for riches.

"If it will help save the company, count me in" Glen sighed sarcastically.

"Sure thing, boss man" Dick chuckled.

"Where's John?" Frosty asked.

"Probably IN the John. He thinks that they named it after him", Dick said.

"It figures", Frosty shook his head. "I wonder if I should put him down for the weekend....?"

"Is it mandatory?" Glen asked.

"No"

"Then forget it. Hey, did you know that his Daddy works up on Mahogany row?"

"Yeah, think I heard something about that. Ten or twenty times. Yesterday..." Frosty acknowledged.

"So fellas, is your break about over?" Frosty asked, looking at his watch again.

"No..." Glen snapped. "Break doesn't start until we're done "talkin' shop" here, boss"

I learned one of my first Boeing lessons. Any business talk with the supervisor during breaks, automatically resets the the ten minute stopwatch back to zero.

Frosty stepped back a few feet, and crossed his arms.

"You can start your break now" he said, getting ready to plant himself there silently, for the next 10 minutes.

This was Frosty's first management assignment. He was a "green" boss, in more ways than one.

Frosty had come out of a "production" shop, where they had "green bars" on their badges. The green meant they had a specified work location, and well defined break and lunch times. Where they were monitored relentlessly, for compliance.

The green men lived on a different planet than the maintenance workers did. Blue badge jobs were looser, and less regimented at that time.

Frosty's looming presence, made all the new guys uneasy. Dick and Glen ignored him, and continued their banter for precisely 10 minutes. Then, Dick rose and said, "Okay boys, Up and at 'em"

"Rick, you wanna spray? Bob, Ed how about you guys scrape the walls?"

He handed me my brand new "Red Devil" paint scraper, a wire brush, and a fresh, virgin putty knife.

Feeling the bosses hot breath blowing down my back from yards away, I scraped the old chipped paint eagerly, like a chipping machine. I was trying to make a good first day impression. Glen and Dick loaded up the paint pot, as Rick prepared his spray gun.

We had got a little head start on prepping when Rick began to "shoot" the walls. Glen was laying out pieces of sheet metal on the tar floor, to shield it from the over-spray.

Dick eyed Frosty in amusement as he stood there rigidly watching, like a statue of a real "boss". Making sure that all his little elves, were all being industrious.

"Hey Ricky...Let me see that thing. That spray pattern don't look quite right to me" Dick said, taking the spray gun from Rick's hand.

He twisted an adjustment screw, and pointed the gun up in the air. Pulling the trigger, it shot a thick cloud of light brown paint high into the air. The sticky fog of paint blocked the sun. Frosty backed away, before the screen of paint descended on his sharp three piece suit, like a swarm of locust.

"Okay, I'll talk to you guys later" Frosty shouted from a distance, backing away from the descending paint. He trotted toward the ladder, As quickly as he had come, he disappeared over the edge of the building.

There was no better "boss repellent" than a thick screen of spray paint. Glen shook Dick's hand, and they both laughed. "You really know how to get rid of a boss"

"Alright guys. We'd better start cleaning up for lunch" Dick decreed.

It was quarter to 11, and we'd already finished our 5 minutes of work before lunch. We splashed our hands with thinner, and dried them with rags to clean up. Everyone opened their metal lunchboxes, and pulled out our sandwiches, as we watched the speedboats bouncing across Lake Washington.

"So, what do you think about this place, Big Ed?" Dick asked with a peanut butter and jelly frosting on his white teeth.

"It's pretty good so far..." I answered. It was FAR from what I had expected.

The previous summer, I had worked for my Uncle Boyd, painting houses Uncle was a perfectionist, and a task master. He expected me to earn every penny of my minimum wage money.

Start, break and lunch times were precise. The pace was brisk. And he demanded flawless results. No drips, no "holidays", and no paint "outside the lines". He didn't believe in using paint rollers. Or masking tape. Uncle was Michelangelo with a house painting brush. And he expected no less from his "helper"

Here at Boeing, I was working for over twice the money. With half the demands. Perfection would have been overkill on painting this rooftop wall, which hardly anyone would ever see up close, nor care about.

The boss didn't lord over us. A brisk pace was discouraged, and stretching the job out to make it last was favored. I was beginning to understand the company's nickname, the "Lazy B"

After lunch, John finally showed up, packing a portable radio, he had tuned into Seattle's top 40 station, KJR.

"I know...it's only Rock 'n' Roll, but I LIKE it..." he sang with Mick Jagger, dancing around on the rooftop like the painting crew's minstrel.

John didn't do much work, he was only there for the ride. Dick would suggest that John help out sometimes. And John would, if he felt like it. He was untouchable.

We finally got down to work. Bob and I scraping paint and priming, working ahead of a couple others who were painting. With powerful state of the art, airless paint pots, it didn't take us much time to cover a lot of yardage.

Rick was becoming flustered by John's carefree, lazy antics. Bob and I didn't care, we were just happy to be there as 18 year kids, bringing in some real grown up money. Glen and Dick were pros with the spray guns, and once everybody finally knuckled down, we laid on the paint earnestly.

"Lets get ahead of the game, so we can screw off later" was the credo.

John would cheer us on with the T-Rex song.

"Get it on...Bang a Gong...Get it on...!" he would encourage. It was either mildly amusing, or strongly irritating depending upon if you were Bob, or Rick. When not singing, John would be complaining about how this job was "shit" Bragging that when he got out of college, he was going to be making some real money.

John never told us what he was studying. Nor did we really care. Whatever it was, it better not require any work ethic. Maybe he was planning on going into politics.

John's anthem was "Time of the Season". He put a special emphasis on these words:

"What's your name? Who's your Daddy? Is he RICH...is he rich LIKE ME?" John really loved that autobiographical line.

Over the course of my career, I met several colleagues who also considered themselves invulnerable, thanks to their parents in high places within the Boeing hierarchy.

My Dad was a second level manager, but he never implied that his position made me "untouchable". He had come from the land of the "green bars", and he had worked in a much more strict work culture the maintenance guys did. He would not be my shield. Dad made it clear, that I stood on my own.

16

I got a glimpse of the green bar world early in my work life. It was a long climb up the roof ladder, so when we needed to relieve ourselves, it was easier just to let loose on the black tar roof. Our streams turned to steam quickly in the summer sun.

Any residual odor of our territorial markings, would be erased, when the roofing crew would seal it in fresh hot tar next week.

But, if we had to do a "number two", we had to descend the ladder to use the indoor facilities, rather than leaving our waste to fossilize on the factory roof.

Inside the hangar doors, it was serious business. Everyone was laser focused on their tasks. You could feel the eyes of the managers with their orange bar badges intimidating the workers who were dutifully sweating away. The orange bars warned, "look out". Orange meant they were "bosses".

The workers were alert for the whistles of break-time. Their trained ears picked them out even over the clanging of machinery. Even while wearing earplugs. These guys lived by those bells. They didn't stop working until they heard them ring. And they made sure they had their tools in their hands, ready to go, when the bells tolled that break-time was over.

Washing my hands and stepping up those many rungs of ladder back to the painting job, I reflected that I was pretty lucky to be doing what we did up here on the roof, rather than doing what they did inside.

The maintenance crew were not company robots. We were free wheeling dudes, making the same money as those inside, but in a more relaxed manner. We didn't even have to punch clocks. Our time was recorded on "Salco" computer cards.

We never got "whistle-bit" at the end of the day. Dick would always call it a day, long before quitting time. So we could get back to the paint shack and clean our equipment. And wind down a bit before going home too.

It was oil based paint was back then instead of today's water based "latex" paints. Boeing stocked paint thinners by the drums, and we used it liberally, to clean our brushes, paint guns, and rollers.

The thinners went right down the sink, through a long stretch of pipe, then dumped out into the Cedar River. We not only helped create some new, colorful fish. But we probably even created whole new species, with extra fins and eyeballs, with the mutations spawned by our chemical encouragement.

Painting those"sawtooth" fascias took a couple weeks. Often working 12 hours days, resulting in huge paychecks.

I worked on my first Fourth of July, The "triple time" holiday pay, was beyond my accounting skills. It seemed inconceivable that my skills were that valuable, or at least that pricey. With the big jingle in my pocket, I felt like Bill Gates.

On the roofs, we would see the Boeing roofers, already hard at work when we arrived each morning. It was pitiful watching them. Sweaty, and gritty, with black tar stains on their clothes, and skin.

They choked on the bellow of smoke, while strenuously raking the hot tar. The earlier they started the better when working on a black roof, spreading boiling tar in the summer heat. There was no singing or laughing on the roof crew. With their boots splashing in hot, sticky, lava, smiles were few.

Seeing them, I felt extra fortunate to be on this easy going paint crew, rather than working with those hapless slaves. Our yoke was light compared to theirs, who were in the same pay code as we were.

I began to sense there was a lot of contrast in the various jobs at Boeing. Some of them, such as mine, were easy, and the demands and expectations were light. Others were physically and emotionally draining, toiling under the sun, or under the gun.

As June gave way to July and August, we traveled throughout the plant. Painted walls, doors, the red and white checkerboard of the airport blast fence, and even cyclone fencing.

We used a bright silver aluminum paint on a big, nappy roller to make the tarnished fences look like new again. I loved the smell of that paint. It reminded me of Ovaltine. But it probably didn't taste as good.

When the summer came to a close, Frosty asked if any of us summer helpers wanted to stay on. Rick went back to school in the dorms, John returned to his fraternity. Bob and I were offered positions as "Maintenance Utility Men" We grabbed the opportunity.

The Maintenance Utility position was a general helper job that allowed us to be understudies under any craft, at a lesser (unskilled) pay grade. For this new job we had to relocate from the shores of Renton's Lake Washington, to the banks of the Seattle's Duwamish River, at Plant Two.

2

MAINTENANCE UTILITY MAN

We thought that Renton was pretty grimy. But Plant Two, made Renton seem spotlessly clean, even sparkling clean, by comparison.

It seemed that all of the worlds dirt, soot, slime, carcinogens, and boogers, were swept into the grounds of this sprawling factory complex. Even if a guy didn't do a lick of work inside, he would emerge at the end of his shift filthy. Just from being inside the gates of Plant Two.

The grease, dirt, and contamination were being generated far faster than they could be blown away by smokestacks, or pumped into the river. The sad, weathered, olive drab siding of the 2-40 building, fit well amid the nearby carbon caked steel mills, along East Marginal Way.

Boeing was famous for making airplanes, but I think their principal product back then, was actually toxic dirt, and foul air. As industrial superheroes for the ecology, we were the valiant men who were fighting for cleanliness.

Bob and I wore the capes, with an "MUM" insignia on our chests. For "Maintenance Utility Men"

Our new boss, Lee, was a sharp dressed man, who resembled Captain Binghamton from McHale's Navy. His three piece suits, with snazzy ties were dark hues of Navy blue. I think that was so that the ambient grime didn't tarnish his smart, businessman appearance. Instead it blended in with the dark fabric.

Lee introduced us to our lead man, who oddly enough was also a Dick. He somehow reminded me of the cartoon character "Deputy Dog". As the lead man for the Millwrights, he had better things to do than to babysit us "helpers". So, he handed us brand new push brooms, and gave us our first orders.

"Just start sweeping. Start right here around the Maintenance shacks, and then just keep going", Deputy Dick commanded, with a sweeping motion of his hands.

It would have taken years to scrub down to clean, bare concrete. But we brushed off the softer, layers of dirt, for days on end. Besides Bob and I, there were a couple more guys joining us on our beautification crusade. Another John, and a guy named Kevin joined the effort.

I don't use many people's last names in this book. But it is noteworthy, that on this cleaning mission, Kevin's surname happened to be "McClean"

Brooms in hand, whether moving or not, were enough to persuade the "big wheels", that you were earning your keep. So, the four of us spent quite a bit of time standing around BS-ing, while gripping our brooms.

No one really cared what we did or didn't do. For Lee, it was about "keeping his headcount" up. Having a lot of underlings, meant power and status to the managers. The practice was called, "Empire Building"

We may come in handy in the future, but this busy work was just a way of "hiding" us. Kept men for a rainy day.. Our brooms were our "passes", that proved we were were gainfully employed.

After a week or so, we had become masters of the broom, but it was taking a toll on our morale. Dick sensed our angst, so he gave us an exciting new challenge.

"Go around the fence lines and pick up all the debris..." Dick loved the word "debris", and he even pronounced the usually silent "s" on the end.

The wind had packed decades worth of airborne rubbish into the grid of the chain link fence. Like garnish among the weed, blackberry sprig, and dandelion salad. In the Plant Two tradition of making missiles and other war weaponry, no living thing that dwelt along the fence line was spared.

"If it's growing, pluck it out, and throw it away" Dick instructed. Vegetation filled our garbage cans. Along with candy wrappers blown in from just yesterday, and ones trapped in the mesh of the fences from years ago.

Some of the hearty wildlife that adapted to survive the toxic environment, such as rabbits or rats, could be found foraging around the garbage dumpsters. But the most common breed of vermin at Plant 2, was the "Dust Bunny" Our travels as MUMs, put us deep in their habitats.

We would sometimes be sent to clean up around the inside air handling units. Boeing was a very specialized workforce. Our heat and duct guys would service the units. But they weren't responsible for the janitorial work on the platforms where the machinery was housed. That's what Maintenance Utility was for.

"I'm not going into that shit-hole, Lee. Get your maintenance utility boys to clean it up"

A twenty minute assault with a shop vac, would take make it habitable for the HVAC guys. And give the four of us, a relatively clean hiding place for the rest of the day.

That's where I discovered the joys of smoking Dutch Master's President cigars. The boys would pass the hours smoking and shooting the breeze. Blowing clouds of blue cigar smoke into the air handling units intakes, to share with the busy beavers who were doing actual work, far below us.

As Maintenance Utility guys, we got a mixed reception from the real, journeyman skilled workers.

MUMs were the jacks of all trades, and masters of none. Some tradesmen would consider us a threat to their craft. because we could legally perform some of their duties. Potentially, we were taking away some of their jobs from them.

But, that also meant we could be USED, to do some of their unsavory, dirty work. Leaving the gravy, and the glory, to them.

"This is a job for the Maintenance Utility Man!", they would declare when faced with some needed, but dreaded grunt work, like jack hammering.

Once, I was told to stand on top of a six foot high block of solidified yellow salt, that had been retrieved from some heat treat tank. And bust it into little pieces below my feet with a 90 pound jack. It was a long, backbreaking day.

Another time, when they wanted to service one of those same tanks, my buddies and I were sent in with little chipping guns to scrape that salt off the walls of the still hot tank (about 100 degrees in there). We toiled all day, under surveillance. So, it wasn't all easy work, and good times.

A plumber, put his piping skills to good use, and built a real working still. Producing a gallon jug with a finger loop on the neck, he shared his bottle of authentic moonshine with us. It tasted like it was about 250 proof. One swig did it for me.

You might have been able to drive home safely with a rich percentage of blood alcohol. But if you could barely walk through the gates, it was sure to raise the eyebrows of the guards. They were always checking lunch boxes for smuggled goods. They were like Homeland Security is today at the airports.

As union guys, we always had each others backs, and no one snitched to management about anything. But long after the statue of limitations had passed, I mentioned the moonshine incident to my supervisor Dad.

Dad had come from the tools, and he lived by the same code of trust that we did. I don't think Cliff Sweeney would never rat anyone out. But he was pissed at ME. Not for the moonshine, but for being so naive about the safety of drinking from a non OSHA approved still.

"What, are you crazy...?" he exclaimed. I knew he wasn't opposed to drinking. He loved his beer as much as any good Irishman does. So at first, I didn't know what got his dander up.

"Why? What do you mean....?" I asked

"If they didn't use the right kind of solder building the still, then drinking that hootch will make you go blind." he said, adjusting his glasses.

Relax Dad, I thought. I haven't seen any maintenance guys swinging their hammers, or sweating pipes, while holding white canes in their other hands.

Their speech may have been a little slurred, or they might have staggered a bit as they climbed out on the girders. But these guys knew what they were doing. And they knew what they were drinking. No blindness ever ensued from tipping the plumber's jug.

Back in the mid 70s, the Boeing stock would take a nosedive, on the day before Christmas vacation each year.

Any hard work done on those days, involved setting up the huge potlucks, with no set start or ending times. And preparing the well stocked, wet bars.

Drinking on Boeing property was clearly in violation of the company rules. That's why your boss would look the other way as you cracked your bottle of Whiskey. And his boss would not watch either, when he took his shot of Tequila. Christmases at Boeing, were extremely merry in the 70s. At least in Maintenance.

T'was the season to be Jolly. For everyone, from the janitor to the CEO. No one SHOULD have been allowed out on the roads after those epic drinking marathons. But at Christmas, it was "be of good cheer" Both at work, and on the streets. No, it wasn't right...but times were different then.

At quitting time on Christmas break, there was as much swerving on the roads leaving Boeing, as there was on the rare snowy days in Seattle. Sanding the roads, wouldn't have prevented our drunken cars from weaving down East Marginal Way, as we started out the most wonderful time of the year.

Gridlock was nasty everyday on the Developmental Center, Thompson Site, and Plant Two corridor. But when it snowed, cars would inch out from the parking lot, to be virtually parked on the highway for hours. Traffic would be doing about 50. That's 50 yards per hour, not miles per hour.

Schools would sometimes be canceled due to snowy weather. But it would take the start of another Ice Age before Boeing would give us an excused absence due to icy roads. I only remember that happening once.

All the shifts for Plant Twos considerable workforce let out at the same time. The mad dash for our cars at quitting time was a rat race. Boeing had built tunnels under the road for workers to safely reach the parking lots. But many of the brave and impatient workers, would race across the Highway, dodging cars instead. I was one of those daredevils.

Once, my game of dodge ball with traffic didn't work out very well. I got ran over by a car. He was peeling out of the parking lot while he had the chance, and he didn't see me coming. His fender struck my leg, and I rolled off his fender, slamming his car hood with my lunch box, as I tumbled off to the curb.

With his panic stricken, saucer sized eyes, he rolled down his window and shouted at me, "Are you okay....?"

I picked myself up, and brushed myself off.

"Yeah, I'm alright, thanks..." I waved.

Honestly, it really wasn't his fault. I wasn't supposed to be jaywalking in the first place. The company had designed safe paths to get to our cars. I had kind of come out of nowhere. Why, I'll bet that if I had been that driver, I would have run myself down too.

I was unhurt, but when the guy saw me the next day in the cafeteria, I decided to have a little fun with the incident, to pay back for the minor inconvenience of him mowing me down.   Albeit, unintentionally.

"Oh my GOD!", he cried. "You're that guy I ran over!. Are you doing okay? Are ya?.... Are ya?" he repeated frantically.

I smiled, "Yeah. Thanks man. I'm fine"

But as I walked away, I feigned an exaggerated limp. My gait creating the impression that he had crippled me. I wished that I'd had worn leg braces, to enhance the dramatic effect.

I glanced back, to capture his sad face of guilt and remorse . But he couldn't see my own chuckle, as I turned my head, and continued on my way.

We maintenance utility guys were often sent out to help with a particular craft. That was one nice thing about this job. We could learn a little about the different trades.

We got a preview of plumbing, carpentry, and the wide scope of duties of a millwright without having to settle upon any of those fields.

Some of the guys would take us under their wings, and share the secrets of their trades with us.

Aside from the skills, I also learned much of the "Boeing Way".

Pace yourself. "Don't work yourself out of a job" Why do on straight time, what can be done on overtime? The sooner you finish, the closer you are to getting laid off"

It takes a village. "Don't steal someone else's job" To replace a pump, it takes a mechanic to loosen the 4 bolts. An electrician to disconnect the wires. And a plumber to connect the pipes.

Many of these crafts, handpicked guys out of the MUM pool to fill their job openings. While we learned, and got paid for it, in an easy going atmosphere.

Maintenance had heat and vent, painting, roofing, janitorial, electricians, plumbers, mechanics, and more to choose from. In the 70s, it wasn't very hard to pick a trade and learn your skills on the job from your peers.

If you showed even a little imitative, the opportunity was there just for the asking. Even if you didn't, depending upon the needs of the companies workforce requirements, they might hand you a bone anyway.

Bob was lucky enough to have spent some time with the machine mechanics, and he graduated to that high paying profession.

I hadn't drawn a very high hand of cards, and I was assigned to a related, but less lucrative field. As a machine tool oiler.

3
LATE NIGHTS, AND OILY DAYS

As a kid, I'd imagined myself becoming everything from a fireman, to a rock star when I grew up. But never had I dreamed that the wheels of fate would put me in a slick job like this. At age 19, I was making my fortune as an Oil Man.

Although it was a slight jump in pay from a grade 3 to a 4, I wasn't an oil tycoon in the Rockefeller / Standard Oil sense. I was just tapping 55 gallon drums of Mobil oil to fill up my oiling cans. Then roaming around the factory to lubricate the wheels of progress, in the industrious machine shops of Plant 2.

While my Maintenance Utility friends were drinking moonshine and smoking cigars in the lofts, I was becoming part of the moneymaking division of Boeing, for a change.

Under the watchful eyes of supervision, the machine shop was cranking out parts as fast as the cutting heads could turn. I helped keep the machines purring, by greasing the wheels as their teeth chewed into the metal. My lead man and tutor was Ralph, Mr. Oilcan himself.

Ralph loved oil. His hands glistened from years of dipping them in the Texas tea. His hair was greasy, and his breath was 30 weight. He never spoke of any personal life that he led.

His favorite topics were the BAC oils, and reading he oil sump sight glasses. I tried to share in his enthusiasm, and make him my role model. But honestly, oiling machinery was nothing more than a job to me.

He was picky about giving each machine it's proper drink. Ralph resembled "String Bean", from the "Hee Haw" TV show. Skinny and lanky, he showed me how to crawl all over the machines. to find the orifices, and put the right oil in the right holes.

His face beamed as he spurted his little spout into the waiting reservoirs, or gurgled a quart or two into the ways. He was visibly disappointed when he saw I didn't get nearly as aroused. As the oil would squirt, he looked more satisfied than the tin man. To me, it was just a job. I found my thrills elsewhere.

It was a regular 40 hour a week route, with little opportunity for overtime. I was like the milkman, but delivering petroleum products, rather than dairy goods. I poured quarts in the resesivoirs of the milling machines, where the giant plates would slide across each other.

Also, I squirted "spindle oil" on the high speed cutter bearings. And pumped grease into the "zerk" fittings. Pretty boring work, in a noisy, stuffy shop. But I got to meet a lot of friendly, interesting machinists in my daily travels.

Some were busy beavers, manipulating the controls by hand, constantly measuring their progress with micrometers.

But for the numerical control, or "NC" operators, the extent of their jobs was to turn a machine on in the morning. And shut it off at breaks and lunch.

After the initial setup of the part, automation did the rest/ It sometimes took a week or better for the program to finish milling the huge parts.

These guys made top dollar, to babysit their machines. Trying to stay awake with a book, while the cutters spit metal chips into tub skids.

And they spit their own chewing tobacco "snoose" on top of those metal cuttings.

"Hey Big Ed....Take a dip. It'll put some hair on your chest" Arnie, a chubby, balding, machinist offered. Shaking a can of Copenhagen smokeless tobacco in my face.

It didn't smell good. Either dripping out from the corners of his brown stained lips, nor straight from the tin. But maybe there was something I was missing. I decided to "be a man", and give it a try.

As my mouth turned brown, my face turned green. I discovered what I had been missing. Nausea. Instead of putting hair on my chest, I think it made what little chest hair I had, fall out.

As Arnie laughed sadistically, I proclaimed the end of that experiment, by spitting my glob of my poison tainted slobber, on top of his own, in the tub skid of steel cuttings.

But my daily visits were the highlight of many of those machine operator's monotonous days. When all you have is another chapter of another Louis L'Amour book, and the obnoxious chatter of an angry Cincinnati milling machine to keep you amused, then your oiling boy becomes your best work friend.

If they had allowed radios at the time, I might not have been so popular. But under the circumstances, your neighborhood greaser stopping by, was as good as it got. But management was eager to wipe the smiles off their faces.

Too much talking was discouraged. They didn't want their guys to forget to flip their machines on several times a day. This was "work". They didn't want anyone to be TOO happy.

I think that's why radios were taboo. As were personal coffee pots. They instead made you buy your java from their vending machines.

This coffee dripped into "Poker" paper cups, each with a unique poker hand. Ironic, since the company rules stated unmistakably, that gambling was prohibited.

But everybody's brother was a bookie in the factory. Football pools reached Las Vegas proportions. And for decades, in almost every shop at Boeing, the "Check Pool" was a big event each payday.

The check pool kitty went to the best poker hand, comprised of the last three numbers of your check number, along with the cents from the check amount. You never got to see the actual check that won.

You had to trust the "honor system". Hoping that the organizer would keep this illegal activity on the "up and up". No wonder I never won.

Early in my career, I discovered that Boeing seemed to like to keep it's employees off balance.

As soon as you were content and comfortable in your job or shift, they would think it was time for a change. My first change was from first to second shift. Moving from machine oiling, to the related field of "coolant change".

We would circulate around the machine shop with a "sucker pump", to pump out the coolant that chilled the hot cutting bits of the machines, from their sumps. And replace it with a new batch of refreshing green, oily water.

Around the same time, my friend Bob, unfortunately was sent to the unemployment line. Through no fault of his own. Spurts of hiring, then layoffs, were as common to Boeing workers as the ebbing tide of Puget Sound.

Cuts in one department, would create a domino effect, as some of those affected had seniority rights to other jobs. And Boeing would back fill them, displacing people in those slots.

Although Bob was a promising new mechanic, and he did a great job, seniority was king. Unless you were one of the few with lower seniority whom the company decided to keep, through exercising their "retention" rights.

The Union hated retentions. But in negotiations, Boeing had twisted their arm into allowing them to keep a small percentage of workers, irrespective of their company time. Anyone who had never been retained, automatically classified the retainees as the "suck ups". Or those with Daddies who had protected them under their skirts.

Of course that accusation was leveled at me from some bitter employees, when guys like Bob were getting laid off, and I was kept on.

But Dad swore up and down, that he hadn't pulled any strings to keep me off the layoff roster. And I believe him. I was in a high visibility position on the Oil Crew, and I did take my job pretty seriously. I think I earned my "stay" on my own.

My neighbors in my new job location, were the "Bulb Snatchers", who changed light bulbs, and the "Filter Crew", who swapped out air filters on the air handling units.

We all shared the same work shack, or "crib" and worked the night "swing"shift. We did our duties when all the big wheels that you had to watch out for, had gone home to for the night.

For all three crews, our "Planned Maintenance Work Orders", had a lot of "fluff" time written into them.

My coolant change work orders, had a "little bit" of spare time in the man hours in case we didn't feel like sweating too much on a hot summer night. But the Filter Crew's work orders had ridiculously generous hours. Far more than enough to accomplish their jobs.

There were a dozen guys on the Filter Crew. Plenty to take care of all the Boeing plants, from Auburn to Everett, with time to spare.

But with only Plant Two's air handling units to contend with, the devil had plenty of idle hands, to find mischief for.

A few guys would go out to change filters, on a rotating basis. Meanwhile, for 8 hours each day, there was a continuous card or cribbage game taking place on the table of the crib. There was a secret trap door, behind a file cabinet that led to a hidden room. Inside was a couple of beds, made out of soft scrapped foam rubber, where a guy could catch up on his sleep.

On any given day, several of those guys would punch in, then take off for rest of the night to enjoy their evenings outside of the company gates. They would return shortly before quitting time, to punch out, and secure their rightful wages for the day.

My coolant change group never had those luxuries. But neither did we have to struggle to get our work orders done. I had the lowest seniority of our three man crew. So naturally I was given the choicest, nastiest, stinkiest sumps to suck and refill.

Being the biggest suckers in the company, we were also responsible for cleaning out the "waterfall" paint booths that would capture paint over spray, in cascading walls of water.

I was rarely allowed to partake in the Coolant Crew's most "gravy" job, which fittingly took place in the company kitchens. That was steam cleaning the filters and hoods of the grills. The most treasured of these jobs were in the "executive dining room".

The obvious perk of this job, was trying out the grill, before cleaning it. The refrigerators of the executive kitchen were filled with select cuts of rib eye steaks, intended to dazzle Boeing's CEOS, and customers.

My colleagues took on themselves the responsibility of testing these steaks to make sure they were fit for the VIPS. As well as making sure that the brandy and spirits, were still good for drinking.

Not knowing whether they could trust me, they kept me out of that loop for a long time. Once they finally invited me to the party, I was too scared of the consequences to indulge. But by then, I think they knew me well enough to know that I would never, "rat them out". Union brothers just don't do that to each other.

Back when it was "legal", I did acquire a lot of criminal skills on that crew. Day shift would often lock and hide the keys of a vehicle that we needed (or wanted), to get around the plant in. So, I discovered how to "hot wire" cars, by jumping the starters and the coils with a short length of wire.

I also learned how to "jimmy" doors, and other ways of sneaking into areas that housed supplies we needed (or wanted). It wasn't really "stealing", as all of these things remained on the Boeing property. But it was great training that might have come in handy if I ever got laid off, and decided to embark on a life of crime.

We explored every bit of the grounds and the catwalks of Plant 2, on our journeys for work, and for pleasure.

There is an underground network of tunnels, that run both across at several spots, and the length of the plant in two runs. Full of steam pipes and electrical conduit, they not only served as "fallout shelters", they also made excellent hiding places.

Long before I became a crane operator (when I returned to the company in the 1980s) I ventured up into Plant Two's "Crane Barn", in my travels.

It was like the Library of Congress with it's carpet of magazines strewn across the floor. There were no Life, Look or Time magazines among the collection. These were the nastiest porno rags ever printed.

These books made Penthouse, Playboy, or even Hustler look like the Betty Crocker Cookbook. Like all the other young guys, I had to thoroughly investigate this filth, to see if it was suitable for the workplace. It certainly wasn't.

But that was none of my business. I would never report this contraband. But instead, I would continue the ongoing investigation from time to time, when the workload was slow.

There was also the tank lines in the 2-10 building on the North property. These swimming pool sized tanks would gurgle and bubble, as they heat treated and chrome plated parts. And also up north, the famous Hammer Shop.

These presses were guillotines that would drop an upper mold weighed down by tons of lead onto a lower mold to form sheet metal, and even heavy plate metal into any shape they desired. They fell with a brutal, and an intensely loud force.

I'd heard tales of workers placing all kinds of items between the molds, like oranges for instance, just for the fun of it. With disastrous results. Rather getting an orange juice, I heard that a guy lost an eye. But this story may have just been more mythical tale of Boeing folklore. There were many.

They say it you want to know if a guy is a hard worker, you should look at his shoes. The wear, or lack of it, shows if they've been working, or sitting around.. Another way was to look at their hands. Not for weathering, but for lack of fingers.

I met a couple guys who had surrendered their digits for the company. One guy had gotten his hand tangled up in a fan belt on a machine, and told me his story as we were working on one just like it..

Seeing only four appendages where five had once been, was a more effective "watch what your doing" lesson, than any safety film.

But sure as the tide rises and falls, another round of layoffs would come crashing in. I was "surplussed" from the Coolant Change crew. The filter team were Maintenance Utility boys too, so, I bumped one of the low seniority filter crew guys out of his job.

Somehow, the job planners got the impression that they were granting too much time on the filter change work orders. They trimmed the hours, and cut the crew in half. How would we ever keep up?

It was actually quite easy. They kept whittling away the crew until at last, I was the one and only filter change guy left to take care of the plant. Remarkably, with the team chiseled down from a dozen guys to just me...I still had a little time to spare as I easily met the schedules.

Soon, another shift in manpower would cast me into the domain of the green badge, production workers. In Sandblast.

4
HAVING A BLAST AT WORK

After coming from my blue badge jobs in Maintenance, it was intimating to walk into the 2-66 building to begin my latest assignment in green bar, "Production". Everyone seemed nervous and edgy in this bustling little building. As though they were cringing for an invisible whip, that was about to fall on their backs.

As I tracked down the column number, and spotted an office isolated by four walls and a small window from the industrial confusion, a little man approached me in a curt, unwelcoming manner. I'd later find out it was Bob.

"Who are you looking for?" he asked in a tone that struck me as, "Why are you just standing there? Whoever you are, and whatever you do, get to work"

"Ivan" I said.

"Well, he's right in there" Bob tipped his head toward the door, with a "get moving" type of gesture. I'd later find out that little man, Bob, was Ivan's little man.

I'd heard of his reputation. "Ivan, the Terrible" was a General Supervisor, like my Dad was. By definition, General's are supposed to be heartless, demanding, work lords. But Ivan and my Dad, were famed as being two of the worst.

Ivan looked like a mobster, with his stern face propped up by his three chins. His thick eyebrows raised, as I walked in. I closed the door, dampening the racket of the noisy shop outside a little. "What do you want?" he frowned.

"I'm Ed Sweeney. I was told to report here" I handed him my reassignment paper in white, yellow, and pink triplicate.

He glared at it, then stuffed his fat hand into his desk drawer. I drew back a bit, not knowing if this Edward G. Robinson looking guy in his menacing office, was reaching for his piece to blow me away. I was relived, when he just produced a pen, and signed the transfer. He waved my copy at me.

"Sweeney...." he muttered. "Cliff's son?"

"Yeah" I replied. Maybe they were buddies, or at least shared a "general" mutual admiration for each other, I hoped.

But my answer brought no joy to his miserable demeanor. He picked up a radio, and summoned Bob, who was only feet away outside of his office door. Godfathers don't get up, when they can just cue up a radio, and summon their goons just as easily.

"Get Vern in here" he said, sourly.

It was less than a 5 minute wait, but Ivan was done with our little chat. He just gave me the evil eye, as we waited on Vern.

"Vern, this is Ed Sweeney, your new Sandblast Operator. He's all yours"

Vern put out his hand and smiled. "Cliff's son?" he too asked as he wrung my hand.

THE LAZY "B"

"Yup" I answered as he opened the door for me motioning me out. Little man Bob, let out a little sigh of frustration at our disturbance. He was trying to fill out his little paperwork, at his little desk.

Vern reminded me of Popeye, not only in his appearance, but with his squinting eyes, and ever present pipe, bellowing little puffs of maple flavored pipe tobacco.

His voice didn't sound like the sailor-man though, and he looked a little older than Popeye too. Vern seemed about ten years too late in retiring. I followed him through this uncongenial shop. And out through the exit doors.

"Where are we going Vern?" I asked, puzzled.

"Sandblast isn't in this building... Come on Sweeney"

He led me about a half a block to a smaller, isolated stand alone building, that hissed with the sound of about fifty simultaneous air leaks. Stepping inside, I saw a bunch of guys laughing over the music of a loud radio playing FM Rock. They were semi busy, masking a bunch of small parts on a gray trailer with white "hundred mile per hour tape".

Wow, a radio, I marveled. You never saw those inside the main factories. But things were different beyond the center of the industrial universe. This building was a "satellite" production shop.

The normal rules of nature didn't take hold in the outer orbits of the main factory. I was also shocked to see and smell a peculator, making coffee on a table. A coffee pot in the shop? I think Ivan would have had little Bob burn these guys at the stake, if he knew what was brewing around here.

The lead man, Rick "E", looked like he'd just stepped off the stage at the Sky River Rock Festival. A bearlike man, with long hair, and a gruff, stringy beard, good natured Rick was a breath of fresh air, in this harsh world of building weapons of mass destruction. Rick was cool.

41

As in much of Plant Two, our purpose there was to construct parts for the Minuteman missile program. We would sandblast parts for the silos that launched these rockets. But not before they were prettied up in the paint shop, with a shining, Royal Blue coat of lacquer.

If you're going to annihilate a whole country of people, lets not add insult to injury with an ugly bomb, they figured. Let's make the last thing they ever see, as beautiful as we can.

After a congenial getting acquainted session with Rick and his sidekick Norm, the double doors of the sandblast booth opened. And three guys who resembled Gothic astronauts, emerged from their latest mission inside.

Their space helmets were black rubber hoods, with long draping aprons attached. With a glass, eye window and an air line with a filter dangling down for breathing. The black hoods made them look a little like "executioners" too.

The sleeves and pant cuffs of their blue coveralls, were taped with white duct tape. The leather on the toes of their boots was worn away by the abrasive blasting, revealing the innards of the steel toes.

The long black hoods and the rest of the getup looked like the costumes of some strange cult. As they removed their ritualistic headgear, I was introduced to Dave and Gary.

Gary was a real serious guy, who viewed the art of sandblasting with reverence. He was a fast, methodical, and thorough blaster. Dave was quite the opposite. Not a serious bone in his body. He had memorized all the comedy routines of Richard Pryor and Robin Williams, and entertained us constantly with his verbatim, spot on impressions.

As we got to know each other, most of the guys (except for Gary) were impressed that I played guitar part time in a Rock band. None of them played instruments, but they were all were all music fans.

And very talented doobie rollers, who frequently fired up their wares at rock concerts.

All but Gary, whose personality was that of a Sand Monk. He didn't care for music, or for small talk. Unless it pertained to sandblasting.

Our "sand" was actually bits of steel "grit" that was blasted out of our fat black hoses onto the scaled, crusty metal of our parts. It sprayed the abrasive grit, with the force of a high pressure fire-hose. Gary taught me to brace the hose against my body with the end in a loop to make our bodies take the thrust of these sand jets, rather than fatiguing our hands holding back the thrust.

The triggers were held down by rubber bands to spare our fingers the fatigue of pressing the switches down during our long sessions of blasting. It was highly illegal, and fool-hearty in the eyes of the Safety department, but those pencil pushers didn't have to spend an hour and a half wearing out their fingers to get a rusty hulk of iron ready for paint.

The booth was a room about the size of half a basketball court. There were thousands of holes in the floor that recycled the spent grit, and sucked it back into the hopper to be shot again.

It was hot and sweaty in the summertime, even with the constant movement of air as the booth vacuumed up the sand. But the constant flow of air into our hoods, brought "some" reprieve from the heat.

To keep from blasting our faces off our badges, before entering the booth, we would toss the badges on top of the "clock", that we used to punch in on our jobs.

Once, someone took Dave's badge and colored in the white letters of our organization with a black permanent marker. An insignificant prank. That was, until Dave lost his badge.

It eventually was picked up by and turned in by someone within the plant. When security saw the badge, the men in black escorted Dave to an intense interrogation, under the lights..

That's because white letters on the badge meant you had no security clearance. But black letters meant you were privy to almost any proprietary top secret security information.

I don't know if they waterboarded him, stuck bamboo under his fingernails, or what they did. But after a couple hours of big anxiety in a tiny room, Dave returned visibly shaken.

But he was grateful that he wasn't secretly executed for treason, and tossed in the Duwamish river with concrete shoes. The two headed fish, developed from Boeing's chemical laced fish chow, would have devoured his carcass in mere days.

We did say goodbye to Dave early however. At lunch, many including Dave, would climb to the rooftop of the 2-40 building, eat their sandwiches, then smoke a joint for desert.

On this fateful day, Dave had forgotten that he had left his "lid" of marijuana inside his lunch box. Leaving the plant for the day, he suddenly realized that he had, at the same time as the Boeing guard did, when Dave opened his lunch box for inspection. So long Dave. Sure gonna miss you, and your Richard Pryor impersonations.

Sandblasting, was not a pleasant job. But it was a profitable profession. While it was only a grade four job on a pay scale that went to ten, the overtime we were forced to work, put us among the highest paid employees of the company.

It could have been worse. Sometimes, we were loaned to our mother shop to help out on the dreaded "burr bench". Day after day, year after year, burr bench "mechanics" had nothing to look forward to but another overflowing tubskid of ugly parts to scrape the rough edges off.

In that thankless job, they were watched continuously to make sure they were busy every minute of the day. Breaks were 10 minutes, not 11. Lunches were 30, not 31. They were expected to clean up on your breaks, not on company time.

Those guys never got any respect or glory. They were just shackled with that miserable "burr-den" for lifetimes. I'll bet they dove into their bottles of "Burr-boun" each night to make it through another dreary day of work.

So, I was always thankful to get back to the roar of the sandblast booths.

Days were long, usually 12 hours during the week, and sometimes 10 hours on the weekend. The money was great, but it wasn't really our choice to spend the majority of our lives panting in the heat with our hoses in our hands. Overtime was required.

As a young guy, it wouldn't stop me from trying to live a life, in the few hours of the day that Boeing didn't monopolize. I was barely 21, and since now I had my official "drinking license", I felt obligated to close down "My Place Tavern" every night until 2 am. Getting to sleep by 2:30, left me a half an hour of sleep, before leaving at 3:15 to punch in exactly at 3:30.

Plus, I had my rock band, Mildstone, and we would rehearse from right after dinner, until I left for the bar at about 9:30 each night. And on weekends, we would always have gigs both Friday and Saturday. My only real night to sleep, was after quitting time on Sundays. During the week, I managed to catch a few winks after punching in. We all did. In our legal resting place, the bathroom.

Our shift may have started at 3:30, but when they pushed guys so hard, they surely couldn't expect them to forgo their potty breaks. So, by 3:45, I'd be nestled in on my regular seat on stall number five, in the restroom across the street.

The place was always packed. And after a quick look at the Seattle Post Intelligencer's comics, and the Mike Mailway column, we all closed our eyes for a while, after the conclusion of our "real" business there was flushed away.

The odors dissipated, as the snoring began. Isolated a building away from the roar of the sandblast, it was a peaceful refuge from the toils of work.

The bosses didn't get in until 7 am. And although I'm sure they knew that not much got done on the overtime, as long as the paperwork all squared, no one cared.

It's never been medically documented, but studies strongly suggest that forced overtime, contributes to irritable bowel syndrome, as well as narcolepsy So, the company was directly responsible for us having to take so long in the john.

On a related note, trips to the medical dispensary were another way to kill a couple hours, and get away from it all.

Meandering in random routes around the plant, we would eventually wind up at medical. And wait in line while others who were escaping the grind of their jobs too, got their antacids, cold pills and band aids.

Whether is was cold and flu season or not, we were all ready for the next "flu" bug to roll around, with an ample supply of company issued medication.

A trip to the tool room in a nearby building, could buy you a couple hours of reprieve from the hot sticky sandblast booth too. Once out of the sandblast building, although the 2-66 was just up the street, sometimes we would get "lost". And find ourselves wandering far from home, in the big 2-40 building.

If we happened to run into Vern, he might puff on his pipe, and ask what we were doing way up here. Our ready answer, was that our local tool room was out of whatever we were looking for. Even if he smelled a rat, he didn't really care.

Of course, talking to Vern or any of the well dressed supervisors was just as acceptable and lucrative as working, anytime. So we all learned the skill of stretching out our conversations with managers, like toastmasters.

The 2-40 building was always bustling with productivity. The workers were as industrious as ants, and forklifts or "Jitneys" as we called them, zoomed through the aisles like they were driving on the Autobaun.

Dust and chemical fumes swirled in the arid air. It looked, smelled and sounded like a real bona fide factory. The 2-40 was the nerve center of the plant, and with all the eyes watching everyone's every move, the work areas were a bundle of nerves. This building had a pulse.

My Dad's tooling shop, was inside the 2-40 / 2-41 complex. And no one made their workers more nervous than Cliff Sweeney. He was a good man, and a good General who kept that fearsome, "Look busy...Sweeney's coming this way", facade alive. He once told me a bragging story, about his powers of intimidation.

Two of his machinists were standing around talking together, while a mill was busy grinding away long chips of steel. One of these guys was the biggest, meanest, scariest looking guy that you had ever seen. His size, made short, stocky Cliff Sweeney, look like one of the seven dwarfs. Probably "Grumpy".

Dad didn't scold them or holler. He just strolled up between the two, lifted his heavy thick eyebrows and asked them, "Does it take two of you to do that....?" And he walked away, his point made, and well taken,

Later that afternoon, that big machinist sheepishly knocked on my Dad's office door.

"What do you need?" Dad asked, looking up from his newspaper.

"I'd like a transfer" the big Ogre said.

"Okay...But why?" Dad questioned.

"B-b-because, I'm a SCARED of you..." the giant quivered.
Like I said, Dad was a good General. In those days, a General's biggest contribution to the cause was to be Boeing's "Fear Factor"

Dad fit the mold well. He was bright and sharp. Nothing escaped his attention. He was knowledgeable. He had done each of these jobs a thousand times on his way up. Dad had a frightening scowl, a sharp Irish tongue, and biting Irish wit, although sardonic.

Dad's tongue had always been a rich supply of colorful metaphors. At home, he peppered many phrases with cuss words. "Do what I say, don't SAY what I say..." could have been his motto. As a kid, if I had talked like him, I would have had the cleanest mouth in town, from getting it washed out with soap...

But at home, I never heard him utter the "F" word. I was amazed that he had apparently never heard that one, and didn't include it in his vocabulary. I think it was because of Mom, that the word was banned, amid all of his "PG" and "R" rated language around the homestead.

But, when I bumped into him at work, and he stopped me to shoot the breeze, man to man...not father to son...I was shocked. "F" was clearly his all time favorite word. Every sentence had at least two of the "F" bombs exploding. I couldn't believe my "F"in' ears!

Like everybody else, he had his family hat, and his work hat. We may have sounded and acted like completely different people in the pews of church on Sunday morning, than we did posturing ourselves among our colleagues at work.

Profanity was just part of the workplace jargon. It meant nothing, and I'm sure Dad wouldn't mind me mentioning how he spoke with a salty tongue in those days. The dialect came with the territory. Just being one of the boys.

Still, as I stood there aghast, listening to the words coming from his mouth, I was exempt from any scrutiny for not working. Because, I was in conference with a freakin' General. It appeared to be official company business, to any nosy onlookers.

Going to "Personnel" was another way to kill some time. It has now morphed into HR, or "Human Relations", but back then personnel was our friend. They were good natured, and only had our best interests in heart. Trying to get you into the job, shift or location of your choice. Disciplinary matters were left to your bosses.

Today, bosses have been stripped of almost all of their powers, and HR is the law, judge, and jury at Boeing. But in those golden days of the Lazy B, Personnel was our chief advocate.

I think over the years, the company has learned that mandatory overtime is rarely cost effective. It is suicidal to morale and good attitudes. And tired, bitter employees are not nearly as productive as happy, balanced workers who are privileged to have a life outside of Boeing as well.

But these things were ironed out through labor negotiations as every 3 years, the union and the company would put on their boxing gloves. And step into the ring at contract time.

5
STRIKE ONE

Calling in sick, didn't always mean that we were deathly ill. Hold the flowers and get well cards until you knew the circumstances.

It could just be a case of the Rainer Flu (too many cans of Rainer beer the night before) Or an eye problem "I just can't see coming into work today". Most of the time, you were just sick of getting up, and coming in so early in the morning. Once in a while, it was even a dental issue.

My brother in law Harry, called in laughing one day, complaining of a toothache. His boss knew good and well, that Harry had a full set of dentures.

But in those times, the company did demand a reason for your absence. You had to make a call to Ivan the Terrible to report your reasons for not showing up.

Usually it was Ivan's little man Bob, who picked up the phone.

"4-66 building, Bob here..."

"Yeah, Bob. Ed Sweeney. I'm sick, so I won't be in today. Put me on sick leave"

"Whatever..." Bob would say, as he hung up the phone, and marked me down as an excused, paid absence. That's the way it always went, I thought.

But one day, I was startled to hear instead, the growling voice of Ivan picking up my call.

I went into my well practiced script. "Umm...This is Ed Sweeney, I'm pretty sick today. Will you please put me on sick leave?" When talking to the "big guy", I'd be more cordial than I was to little man, Bob.

"What's wrong with ya...?" the big ferocious boss questioned, skeptically.

I wasn't ready for an interrogation. This wasn't part of the routine. His question caught me by surprise, and I was still groggy. I started naming off every symptom that I could think of.

"My head hurts, I have a stomachache. Terrible chills. I'm running a fever. I have diarrhea, and constipation"

In the confusion of my ad lib, I had accidentally stammered out that I had both.

"My joints hurt, my eyes are red, and I feel faint too...."
I continued, in the most dramatic, "critically ill", weak voice that I could muster.

That should have covered it.

"Boy, sounds like your pretty sick. I don't want you coming back in here, until you bring me a note from your doctor, Sweeney" I guess he didn't want to infect the whole shop.

Oh shit! I was healthy as a horse, just dead tired. What doctor was going to sign me off? I wondered. Surely not mine. I guess my career is over, I trembled.

I never got my doctor's note to give to Ivan. Luckily, I punched in, and managed to dodge Ivan the next morning. And, it just happened to be the day when everyone took off before lunch, for the big strike vote at the Coliseum.

On any other day, at work or at home, these thousands of men and women were just normal, everyday working folks. Calm, decent, happy people, just trying to put some bread and butter on their tables.

But as the Union speakers lathered the crowd into a frenzy, the throngs metamorphosed into an excited, drunken mob of agitators. Screaming for a revolution.

"Strike, strike, strike!" they all bellowed. So loud, that no one could what the speakers were saying about the contract issues we would be voting on. Obviously, they must have been pretty bad. Plainly, there was going to be a strike, at the conclusion of this vote.

This was 1977, and it was my first experience with strikes. I would become an old hand at waving a picket sign by the time I retired in 2016.

As in every strike, a percentage of the membership had voted to turn down the contract proposal based upon what they thought were valid issues.

Another faction of the "nay" votes, rejected the contract just to get a breather from the continual overtime that they were forced to work.

Others would vote no on any contract, no matter how good or bad it was. Just because they enjoyed the tradition of striking, and of "standing up to the MAN"

Although my Dad was a second level manager, he had been a shop steward before he had worked his way up the ladder. Nobody had more heart for the Union's solidarity, and devotion to get a fair shake for the workers than Dad.

If I ever crossed a picket line, I would be no son of Cliff Sweeney's anymore. Being a "scab", was never an option for anyone from this proud, tough Irishman's family.

Dad often lectured about the many reasons that the Union deserved my allegiance. He was there in the early days, before the company had decided that hourly workers deserved any benefits or perks.

When my Dad was a young man, they had vacations. But they were unpaid. And they were required to take the time off. Boeing recognized the need for a little breather once a year, but didn't consider the financial impact on a struggling family, to be docked for taking that leisure time. Strikes brought this inequity to the companies attention.

Medical and dental were the employees own problem, before the Union made the company take an interest in the health and well being of their employees.

There is much anti-union sentiment these days. But there is also a lot of ignorance regarding what unions have done to better the middle class of everyone. Regardless of union affiliation, the sacrifices made by union workers, raised the bar for every future worker, represented or not, and actually created the middle class.

Back in the industrial revolution, factories were divided into two camps. The privileged higher echelon Kings and Bishops, and the low class peasants or pawns. The sweat of these low paid, mistreated workers earned the prosperous aristocrats their wealth.

Meanwhile, the workers themselves lived just above poverty. And toiled for years in unsafe, unpleasant conditions, with no retirement to ever look forward to.

Brave men grouped together to challenge this presumption of the superiority of those factory gods. And demanded that they receive more equitable treatment for their labors that made the bosses their riches.

In those early times, it wasn't merely a negotiation, and a battle of words. It was a war. Some were even killed on the picket lines fighting for workplace justice.

As the workers banded together and stopped production, companies were forced to take the demands of the workers seriously. Respect for the blue collar workers, wasn't given benevolently from the kind hearts of management. It was earned through sacrifice, just as earnestly, as were their poverty wages were earned before these uprisings.

I don't fault the factory owners for wanting to squeeze as much as they could from their employees, for as little as they would have to give them. It's the nature of success in free enterprise, to be greedy, and hard nosed.

They were doing a good job, by using cheap labor to make big profits. Company interests were only interested in company interests, not in the feeding the of mouths of those who work for them.

Likewise the Union was doing exactly what they were supposed to do by raising a little stink to blow into those hard noses. By being the squeaky wheels, they indeed eventually got greased. Healthy companies with a happy work-forces were born in the balance of these opposing forces.

By the time I rolled around, the Union would ask for the moon, as the company stood their shaking their heads, with folded arms. Over the course of a strike when the profits fell, and the workers savings were exhausted, the company would unfold their arms. and offer them tasty "moon-pies", in lieu of the acreage in the Sea of Tranquility that they had asked for.

The workers would hungrily take the pies. And the company brass would return to their offices and close the doors. And we'd all be happy, until we would meet again in another 3 years.

But in 1977, after we had cast our negative votes, the throng of workers kept chanting "Strike" as we marched off the grounds of Seattle Center. Sweeping the sidewalks with the cuffs of our bell bottom jeans.

The smokestacks would smolder, and then die out, as burn barrels lit up outside the gates of the Boeing plants. We waved our picket signs at the cars who would pass by.

Some would honk at us. And in return, receive our smiles and acknowledging shakes, from our signs. Others would give us the thumbs down, and be answered by our cussing, and angry waves of our middle fingers. We were all about community relations.

Mother nature saved up her nastiest, rainiest nights of the decade for our strikes. I recall one strike, where it was so stormy that hardly anyone showed up for their midnight strike duty. But I was there. I was a "sucker".

I was dropped off alone, at the corner of East Marginal way and 16th Avenue. The monsoon was so fierce, that it kept most cars off the road on that lonely night.

Although traffic was exceptionally light, the occasional car zipping by would raise big waves from the curbside mud puddles, to splash my already drenched clothing. The burn barrel sizzled, as the downpour put out it's last embers.

At least the van from the Union hall would be coming by soon with hot coffee and the Aero Mechanics district 751 official strike food staple, the egg salad sandwich. Or so I thought. They usually came by every hour.

I can imagine the argument among the drivers in the union hall, as I stood shivering and waiting, in the pounding rain.

"I'm not going out there...It's too wet. YOU go..."

"No way, I went last time....It's YOUR turn...."

"Listen, lets just calm down, and have a cup of coffee and think about it..."

For the next 4 endless hours, no one came. I quivered in the darkness and chill as I became one with the rain. My nose ran as I coughed, and fought against hypothermia.

"We had BETTER get a good contract" I sniffled to myself. "I'm sure EARNING it ", I thought.

At the end of the night, the van finally pulled up. The driver jumped out, dry, warm and smiley. "Oh, sorry man, had a little car trouble", he lied, with a chuckle.

I hoped in the van, as my replacements picketers filed out. And I grabbed my overdue, hopefully still good egg salad sandwich. My hands were so numb, that I couldn't even feel the bread in my frostbitten fingertips.

NOW, I could have gone to the doctor, and gotten a legitimate sick note for Ivan the Terrible. I really was sick, this time. Sick of the rain. Sick of my $50 a week strike paychecks. And just plain sick, sick. Bed sick.

On some strikes it was so disorganized that we would earn our $50 weekly pay, just for waiting in line for our strike checks. I recall one of those times at Longacres racetrack in the 1980s, when the exasperated workers almost struck against the Union, as we waited all afternoon for our pay.

But all of the picket lines weren't so bad. I remember in the 1990s, at Thompson Site on East Marginal way, it was almost like a party. A rowdy bunch of guys, having a great time barking our injustices to the busy traffic. Harassing the supervisors and scabs who were driving through the gates.

Pallets were nailed together, creating homey little shacks to wait out the weather in. When it didn't rain, the smells of barbecue would be flavoring the air.

The Thompson site was my home plant. And I was ashamed that it was also the scab capitol of Boeing at the time. Many friends turned into enemies, as those who didn't embrace our cause, waltzed across the picket line.

Once the strike was over, you could get fired for harassing these "November Workers" But we sure gave them a piece of our minds, as they crossed the gate while we were holding our signs.

Personally, I always felt that I didn't know everyone's circumstances. While it was troubling that we couldn't all group together to get a better deal, I tried my best not to judge. Although, I would never cross a picket line, maybe some of them, really had to.

But others were just disrespectful and arrogant, as they would spit on our cause. Fearing retaliation, Boeing would bus the scabs into the Thompson site from some secret, undisclosed pickup location. One guy in particular, really stirred the hornet's nest, as the bus left the plant.

I knew Lou, who was a production mechanic, when I ran cranes as PSD. I'd thought he was a decent guy. But hearing that he had smiled and stuck his tongue out at my Union brothers, made me reconsider my opinion of him.

Even worse, I heard as he was sitting safely in the scab bus, he had pressed his big scab paycheck against the glass, while flipping off the picketers, with his free hand.

In the 2000s, most of my crane colleagues were united in respecting the picket line, but a couple of them crossed the line.

That year, my wife and I had just closed our gift store, "Sunny Day Gifts". The store had been unsuccessful, and had rang up a ton of debt.

At contract time, I was just beginning to consult with an attorney about filing bankruptcy. I had a "shut off notice" from the power company, that I had no way of paying. And we were about to go vote on a contract, that was sure not to pass.

A friend from work, Pat, told me, "Eddy, I won't blame you if you have to cross the line" He knew my circumstances. But I made it clear that I would never cross my union's line. I'd still be in a world of hurt financially whether I crossed or not. But by going out on strike, I'd still be able to look myself in the mirror. And look in my Dad's eyes.

The strike came and went, and for those who felt they needed to cross, I tried to forgive and forget. But then a colleague was showing me pictures of his sharp new Harley. I was impressed, until he shared the story of how he got it.

"That's my STRIKE BIKE" he said proudly. He had purchased it with the proceeds of his massive overtime checks, while we were standing out in the rain, getting him a raise for the future.

I'd always liked this guy, but it was disturbing to hear. If I had commented on what I thought about it, that would only earned me a trip to HR. And possibly a one way ticket out the gate. So I left it alone.

It was a hard lump to swallow though.

Although management despised strikes, they really did help build a camaraderie among it's workers, that often translated into a real team spirit. Sacrificing together and working toward a common cause, also helped build teamwork that would be used on the job.

And enhancing pay and benefits would also make the demanding times more worthwhile for us. A happy, well paid workforce is easier to motivate than a cheap, unappreciated group, I would argue.

After that first strike in 1977, we were anxious to return to our jobs and paychecks, although we had gained some fond memories of striking together for our common good.

As expected, Ivan had forgotten all about my doctors note, as I put on my hood and blasted away the rust form the parts, and the bitterness over the labor dispute.

6

LOOKING BEYOND THE SANDBLAST BOOTH

It didn't get any easier working in Sandblast after the strike. Not only was there plenty of overtime trying to catch up for lost time during our work stoppage, but my rock band was really starting to cook too.

We all had our sights set on quitting our jobs and becoming professional musicians. Our nightly rehearsals and weekly gigs took up virtually all of my spare time. I even had to cut down on my drinking time in the bars.

Plant Two had two sandblast booths. I normally worked in the smaller one, in the 2-70 building, near the Duwamish river. But I also spent some time in the larger booth, in a place called the "Camo" building, just off East Marginal Way.

It's an interesting story, how the Camo building got it's name. It used to house a bunch of props that they used in World War 2 to disguise the buildings of Plant 2 to resemble a residential neighborhood.

The rooftops would have what would like like streets, housetops, even shrubbery and dummies to look like children playing in the streets. In the hopes that the Japanese bombers would become confused looking for our factories and retreat.

After the war, this building became a large paint booth, with it's neighboring building becoming the sandblast booth. Sometimes us sandblast guys would be told to come and help mask parts for the paint booth. Other times I would have to blast the missile silos, in the big booth.

No matter what I was called to do, the guys on this side of the plant always seemed pretty up, and energetic. Especially a painter named Robbie. We were all working long hours. How did these guys manage to keep so spry? I wondered.

It didn't take long to discover the extra ambition didn't come naturally. It was through the wonders of modern chemistry. As soon as they decided that I could be trusted, they let me on their secret potion.

Coffee just wasn't doing the trick anymore. My chronic fatigue was taking it's toll both inside and outside of work. Robbie noticed me half dead, slowly taping and plugging the missile silo he was about to paint.

"Man, you look beat. Try a couple of these..."

He held a few tiny little white pills, with lines going across both directions in his hand.

"What is it?", I yawned.

"Criss cross...", he percolated. "It'll make you feel like a million bucks"

They scared me. Aside from a little pot, which I wasn't crazy about either, I was leery of illicit drugs. "Thanks, but no thanks", I declined.

I happened to mention it to the guys in my band at rehearsal that night. They were enthusiastically in favor of me giving myself a little "pick me up". Truly, I needed it.

"Come on Sweeney, it's not hard drugs. They just give you a little more energy. You don't even get high off them. They'll just help you stay awake, and really come alive. Try them. You'll like it. You need it. Don't worry."

So, the next day, I approached Robbie and asked if the offer was still on. "Sure" he said. "And if you need some more, I'll sell you this whole bag for five bucks"

Reluctantly, I downed them, and for the next couple hours I was the employee of the day. Feeling good, energetic, I was masking parts like the masked man. No side effects, no stoned feeling. Just feeling good, strong, and ready to work.

I pulled out a five dollar bill, and bought the "nickel bag" from Robbie.

For the next week, I was Boeing's "Master Blaster", and the envy of the paint prep world. "How overrated sleep is", I thought. I was alert, happy, and ready to work 24 hours a day for the whole week.

Then, suddenly as I stood in the sandblast booth, all of my energy left me at once. Like a balloon that had been popped with a pin. My whole body slowed, with the exception of my heart, which was beating away like a rabbit.

And then, I felt my nerves telling my heart, "Come on buddy, beat! Beat faster" My heart was replying, "No way man, I just can't keep going like this..."

I was really frightened, and I had no idea what to do. I was probably going to die at age 22 right here in the sandblast booth.

I felt like I needed help, but if I asked for it, I'd probably get fired for taking drugs. So, I just waited it out for the next hour. I slowly returned to a very, very tired version of normalcy. I never touched amphetamines again.

But making it through without sleep, almost took my life another way, without substance abuse. In the midst of another grueling week running on only a few hours of shuteye, my eyes decided they could no longer stay open. Unfortunately, I was driving down East Marginal at about 45 miles per hour at the time.

The car horns blasting at me was the most effective alarm clock that I'd ever heard, I awakened, swerving back to my lane just in the nick of time to avoid a deadly head on collision.

I decided right then and there, that job or no job, I would never get behind the wheel if I were that tired again.

I jumped at the chance, when Vern offered a short term transfer to graveyard shift. I'd always been a night-owl anyway, but I could sleep in the daytime while the guys in the band were working.

Then I could wake up refreshed, and go through our rehearsals. And work my short shift with only a fraction of the sleep deprivation that I had been enduring. (Graveyard was only a 6 and a half hour shift, compared to the 8 hours on day-shift)

It worked well in those respects, but the problem was the band always had performances on the weekends. And Boeing always needed overtime to start at midnight on Fridays and Saturdays.

This conflict of interest got me a "CAM", or corrective action memo. If you got three of these in a year, you were out the door.

Going "out the door", was part of the agenda for the boys in the band, anyhow. We would never become rock stars just playing on the weekend nights, and carrying our lunch boxes into the factories each morning. But, we weren't quite ready to kiss these well paying jobs goodbye quite yet.

Boeing looked down on Moonlighting. If you worked there, you were married to Boeing. And outside employment was looked upon like adultery. So, I soon found my way back to the exhaustion of day shift.

But working in a hot hellhole like sandblast, made it easier to cut the umbilical cord, when we finally reached our big "quit day" in 1979.

The guys I worked with were great, and the pay was outstanding. But Sandblast wasn't really the kind of job that you would enjoy for a lifetime. Except for guys like Gary.

I told you about Gary in the last chapter. The sandblast monk, was not only committed to the cause, he was also the fastest blaster in the world.

"You got to get a routine down, and keep that hose moving..." he would constantly instruct me.

While I understood, I just couldn't do what he did the way he did it. Sandblasting was tremendously boring to me. So in the process of spraying away the rust, I would sometimes draw funny pictures in the rust scale that I was blasting off the metal with my blast hose.

I don't mean to brag, but some of them were true masterpieces, if I don't say so myself. Gary would finish his half of the parts long before me, and come over and erase my genius artwork, eager to get the next load into the booth.

Some people just don't appreciate fine art. Or share my sense of humor. Gary was one of those.

If I wasn't in the hot booth blasting away, I was outside prepping the next trailer load for blasting. It's a wonder that none of us exploded.

That's because almost everybody smoked cigarettes then. In fact cigarette machines were scattered around the factory. As we loaded up rags with the highly explosive keytone to wash grease off the parts before masking, we usually had a cigarette dangling out of our mouths.

It's only by dumb luck that none of us ever ignited. The fumes were so thick though, that much of our prep time was spent being stoned on the keytone.

If we had a nickel for each brain cell we lost in the haze, we'd all be rich. And brilliant.

Sandblast wasn't a very healthy place to work either. They told us that the triple filtered shop compressor air we breathed was safe and wholesome. But they also required us to have chest x-rays every couple of years, to see how our lungs were holding up.

We all had brown underwear too.

Not brown in the way that most underwear gets stained. The steel grit that passed through our taped up coveralls would rust in the washing machine.

We were warned to not use our home washers on our work laundry, because the grit would ruin the washing machine seals. So many of us used a little of our short free time, to go to the laundromats.

Considering everything about Sandblast, I felt working there was a mixture of blessings and curses. I was blessed, that I avoided the layoffs that had made many others become unemployed. I was blessed, with great wages and benefits. I was blessed, with a good crew of guys that was easy to work with.

But I was cursed, in a dirty, thankless job in hot coveralls, locked in a hotter work area for hours. I was cursed, to working mandatory, forced overtime, and fighting continual exhaustion.

I was cursed, with ring around the collar from rusty steel grit. And I was cursed with boredom and monotony in a job that no one really cared for. Except Gary.

The blessings made it a hard job to quit. The curses made it an easy job to leave. The stalemate was broken by my dreams of making it big with my Rock 'n' roll band. In my band, we all decided on a quit date to turn in our badges, and pursue our rock n roll fantasies.

My friends at work cheered my decision, wishing me luck on this pursuit. My Dad was skeptical, but didn't want to be the one to burst my bubble. So, he said very little.

My band mates had convinced me to ask my parents if I could move back home to save money. We expected some lean times on our way to making millions. Reluctantly, I agreed to move back to my old bedroom at home. Mom was ecstatic. Dad rolled his eyes.

So on November 5th 1979, after working for 5 years and 4 and a half months, I resigned my Boeing job. Expecting to never look back, nor go back.

7

THE REAL WORLD

We've all heard the expression, "The grass is not always greener on the other side" Leaving Boeing, I learned that indeed the grass was greener outside than it was inside of Plant Two. Where they killed anything that grows. But green grass doesn't always mean more money, or a higher standard of living.

Since this is a book about working at Boeing, I'm not going to spend too long describing my next five years as an ex Boeing employee. But I will quickly run through the highlights. There were some big highs. Big money, was not part of those highs.

Mildstone didn't want to be a club band. We wanted to be the Rolling Stones, playing concerts. While we did some week long engagements along the way, we mostly kept to one nighters on the weekends at first. Using the time during the week to hone our "concert" act.

I ran through my accumulated 401K savings quickly, being accustomed to the luxury of my Boeing wages. It took me a while to grasp the disparity between my old Union wages, and my new share of $600 a week, split 4 ways.

Working a couple of nights a week, and after subtracting expenses and paying our road crew, I was lucky to make 50 or 75 dollars a week.

It was a blast, being little rock stars, and playing music for a living. The applause and excitement that we got from our audiences were a reward unto themselves. But cheers and notoriety, didn't pay the bills. Soon, I had to sell my beloved brand new Boeing Credit Union financed pickup truck, to make ends meet.

Personally, I liked playing clubs, because it put close to $200 a week in my pocket. And, I actually enjoyed traveling and living out of a suitcase in a hotel room.

The rock bands who complained about how hard it is "on the road", had never spent 12 hour days in Sandblast. Or jack hammering blocks of yellow salt all day. Relatively speaking, playing guitar and singing, was a "piece of cake".

We never toured to make an album like "Made in Japan" as Deep Purple had done. But we did play our music in hundreds of places throughout the Northwest and Canada. The crowds seemed to love our "Pure Energy Rock", as our slogan had touted our music as being.

The closest we came to being "Rock Stars", was playing in the legendary Paramount Theater in Seattle. The last performer to use our dressing room before us, had been Tom Petty. Our after performance sweat, blending with Tom's lingering perspiration, was our closest brush with the big time.

We had picked a real bad time to start making our livings in live entertainment in the first place.

Disco was the latest thing, and many venues had stopped hiring bands in favor of disc jockeys, playing Bee Gees and KC and the Sunshine band records. It really cut into the opportunities for small time rock performers. If only we'd been born five years sooner.

As the money supply got tighter and tighter for me, I would sometimes be surprised by learning there would be no pay at all this week. As we had needed an equipment upgrade to stay competitive. Rather than our measly, meager paychecks, I'd find we had purchased new Shure Microphones instead. All fine and well, except I can't get much nutrition from eating my new mike.

To keep our heads above water, the boys in the band took on odd jobs, here and there. Some of our more mechanical players, would find beat up cars rotting in the brush in people's yards. They would buy them for next to nothing, put in a little elbow grease, and a tune up, and make hundreds of dollars on a resale.

But for me, being one of the world's worst mechanics, I went rolling off into the ditch instead. To try and scrounge up some aluminum cans, to recycle and keep myself solvent.

I also tried doing some phone sales at the Seattle Times newspaper. Only to discover that I was an even worse salesman, than I was a mechanic.

I think the last straw for me, was trying to bleed my way into a few bucks in my wallet. I walked into the "Plasma Center", ready to roll up my sleeves, and sell a little of my life blood to supplement my rock and roll riches.

Looking around at my fellow donors in the waiting room, I felt out of place. I was neither a wino nor a junkie like the rest of the Plasma guys were. That was it. "I've got to get a JOB", I told myself.

For years to follow, I would be recognized by some stranger in a Kmart, or on the street. "Hey you're that guy from Mildstone, aren't you?" They would say. "I saw you guys at...(wherever)" I guess we did leave a little impression.

After nearly 2 years of living and starving in my rock and roll lifestyle, I wished the guys in my band good luck, and got into making some real money. Working at 7-11.

It was in the spring of 1981.

Well, it wasn't GREAT money, but it was a huge raise over what I was making as a "rock star". I actually loved the work far more than anything I had done at Boeing. Free coffee, soft drinks, and Slurpees. A nice walk in cooler to chill out in on hot days. Air conditioning. A nice blend of regulars to banter with everyday.

If the pay and benefits had been better, I probably would have spent the rest of my working days there. The store was right in my old stomping grounds, in Tukwila.

I got to see many people that I'd grown up with on a regular basis. Pretty girls in slinky bikinis would come in and flirt, while I got them their hot dogs and Slurpees. The bosses were pretty nice too.

They did expect us to keep busy all the time. They had one of the nicest 7-11s in Seattle, and demanded housekeeping, stocking and facing of shelves when not busy. My experience at Boeing had never been as strict as it was here at the convenience store. But I never minded working hard. I'd always had the "When in Rome, do as the Romans", outlook on work.

But they had had some "shrinkage" as they called it. The tills weren't adding up right. It certainly wasn't me, but being the new guy, I was the first that they let go.

As I picked up my final paycheck, I emphasized to my boss that I'm not a thief, and I would hope they would consider me for reemployment in the future. Eventually, they did rehire me. But in the interim, I worked a couple other jobs.

I did a stint as a enumerator for the US Census Bureau. My job was to track down addresses of those who hadn't completed their 1980 census forms, and come back with the skinny on who lived there.

The first door I knocked on was friendly and cooperative. "Come on in man...Have a seat. Hey, you wanna smoke a joint?"

Of course I couldn't. Nor did I want to. I was there on official US business. But, it was awfully nice of him to ask.

Later that month, on one hot afternoon, I was offered a cold beer, as I helped someone else complete their census form. This time, I did accept their gracious offer, on behalf of the United States of America. It was refreshing to meet so many friendly Americans. Especially when they were offering cold brews, on a scorcher of a day.

After that, I became one of those survey takers that you sometimes tried to dodge at a department store, when you saw us coming at you wielding a clipboard.

Many marketing research companies insisted that their "field interviewers" closely follow the annoying scripts printed on the survey forms. And paid hourly wages for the interviewers to go through dozens of, "No"s, before finding someone to agree to their probing.

My company, Wade West Marketing research, didn't give a hoot HOW we got the information, as long as we got it. They got paid per completed verifiable survey, and they paid us well for the piece work too. So I tossed the script, and would cut to the chase.

"Hey, do you like to eat candy bars?" I would ask. If they gave me a yes, and seemed to fit the demographic that I was looking for, I'd offer them a deal. "Look, if you give me 5 minutes to answer a few questions, I'll give you 5 bucks, okay?"

I might get paid 15 or 20 dollars for my completed form, so I just made it worth everyone's while. I'd whip through the questions, get their validation information and have them on their way as promised, cash in hand. Then on to my next customer, until I reached my quota.

I had learned at the Seattle Times, that I couldn't sell Boy Scout cookies to my own Grandmother. But with a little bribe, and some fast talking, I could get most anyone to give me their name and phone number, and tell me why they loved a Snickers bar.

But there was nothing like the security of a regular paycheck at 7-11. Thank heaven, they eventually found the culprit that had been ripping them off, and rehired me, with a raise at my familiar store, in 1983.

This time around though, I decided to pursue an education in a field that I might like, while working full time at the store.

People had often told me that I had a great voice, and I also loved music and creative writing as well. So, I signed up for some expensive tuition, at the Ron Balie School of Broadcast.

Almost like back in my old Sandblasting days, I was extremely busy all the time. I was either working, or going to school or both, 7 days a week for the next 9 months.

I did very well in my classes, and I graduated near the top of my class.

Balie had bragged about their "98 percent job placement record", and shortly after graduation, they called me with a job offer.

"Hey, do you want to work PART TIME running the disco at a Chinese restaurant in West Seattle for minimum wage?" they asked me.

"Yeah right...", I thought. After spending a fortune on tuition through student loans that I'd be paying off forever, I'd rather be jack hammering giant cubes of yellow salt, than accepting this cheesy, insulting job offer.

"No thank you", I replied. "I'll tell you what. Change your placement record to 97 percent. And don't call me anymore" I said, concluding my relationship with my Alma mater.

I did do a brief, unpaid internship at the smallest AM radio station in the world. The unknown, un-liked station, KSCR in Renton as the morning newsman. With ratings so low, that they couldn't be measured,. But, after a few shows, the station manager decided he didn't like what I was doing, so he canned me.

74

My Dad asked me, "How's it going at the station....?"

"Ah, they let me go Dad...."

"What's the matter, were they paying you too much...?" he sneered sarcastically. He knew it was an unpaid position, and he didn't mean to insult me. He was just kind of pissed at the manager for letting me go so fast. But Dad's comment still kind of stung.

"Well son, are you ready to go back to a real job? You want me to see what I can do?"

I sighed, "Yeah, okay Dad. Thanks"

Dad made a call to his friend in Personnel. And like magic, I went to the front of the line for a job interview. Kind of like an episode of Mr Wizard.

"Drizzle, Drazzle, Drozzle Drone...Time for this one to come home"

Back home to Boeing again.

8

BACK TO WHERE I ONCE BELONGED

On October 8th 1984, 4 years, 10 months, and 28 days since I had resigned from the Boeing Company, I found myself inside the gates of their Kent Space Center. Mulling around a construction site.

"Oh Boy", I chuckled to myself. "Here we go again" Since I'd had some experience, it was easy to slip me back into my old job. I was once again, a Maintenance Utility Man.

But things had changed since the last episode. Plant services had two faces. One side was maintenance. The other was construction. I was an official "grunt" on the GCU crew. GCU stood for the General Construction Unit.

Since we were building structures right out in the open for everyone to see, there was no "hiding" here. Under the watchful eyes of the production shops, our own management and the great and terrible "Superintendent" of the Space Center, it was no nonsense work.

Dan was my new boss, and he brought me out to introduce me to the skilled craftsmen on the crew. "Bob, this is Ed...our new man"

Bob shook my hand. "What's his craft?" Bob asked Dan while wringing my hand.

"Maintenance Utility" Dan answered.

Bob handed me his shovel. "So, why am I doing this?" he asked Tim.

It was time for the grunt to start grunting. Bob and Dan stood B.S.ing for the next hour as they watched me finish digging the hole that Bob had started.

As the new laborer on this assignment, I spent the next few jobs, being everybody's "boy". Relieving all the skilled guys by taking on every strenuous, backbreaking dirty job that they would rather not do. The construction guys were happy to have me on board. Things really had changed.

The money had changed a little bit too. Back in the 70s, it only took months to work up to your top pay under the "Learner Progression Program". Now, it took 6 years, with the increases split into 12 small jumps at 6 month intervals.

But I'd changed too, since I was last at the Lazy B. While it was a comedown from my lofty ambitions of being a rock star, the pay and benefits were awesome, compared to my compensation out there in "the real world"

I was grateful for this second chance to make some real money. And being the low man on the totem pole, I really dug in, both in and out of dirt holes, to make a name for myself.

Vocationally, I'd spent the last few years as a drifter. Now back at Boeing, I was instead a "floater", constantly reassigned, to where I was most needed. No one needed me worse than "Willie"

"Hey Willie, come here", Dan called to this scruffy little millwright across the factory bay. Willie pretended to ignore him, as though he couldn't hear over the clamor in the noisy shop. Actually Willie had heard. He just didn't like to be told what to do. In his own sweet time, Willie strolled over to see what Dan wanted.

"Meet your new helper, Ed" I shook hands with this grubby little guy. He was barely 5 feet tall, missing a finger, and had an uncanny resemblance to the "Frito Bandito" His enthusiasm was immeasurable, as he shook my hand, limply.

"Go do whatever Willie tells you to do", Dan ordered.

"Come on kid", Willie motioned as he walked away.

"Where are we goin'", I asked.

"To get ready for the job" Willie mumbled.

I followed him away from the construction site, up some stairs. Then, up a ladder into some isolated rafters of the building. Walking along a little catwalk, he led me to a landing, with a couple of chairs on a diamond plate metal floor. He pulled out a joint.

I'd only been back to Boeing for a couple days. I nervously looked around for spying eyes, or a camera. This was making me edgy.

"What are we doing here, Willie...?" I asked.

"Like I said, getting ready for the job. Here, take a hit..." he offered me the doobie.

"No thanks" I answered. I really hadn't smoked the stuff for years. If I was going to, I think I would have rather done it on my own time, in my own place. An unwanted high was nothing that I treasured above keeping my new job, and making a good impression.

Willie looked let down. "Come on man, take a toke. What, are you, a 'narc' or something?"

"No, you go ahead Willie. I don't care. I really don't like getting high, plus I'm just starting out here. I don't want to do anything that I might lose my job over..."

I hoped that he'd understand my apparent rudeness.

Willie took another hit, and shook his head. "You want to do a good job, huh?"

"Yeah, I do"

"Well, what did the boss tell you to do?"

"Help you", I responded.

"No...He told you to do whatever I tell you to do. And I'm telling you to take a hit..." he laughed.

Against my better judgment, I took a drag on his joint, and handed it back to him. I continued to gaze around the rafters, looking for a spy cam.

After he took another hit he handed me the roach.

"Thanks, but that's enough for me", I declined.

Willie laughed heartily. "One Toke Eddy, that's what I'm going to call you from now on..."

Killing the roach with one last hit, he stood up. "Let's go, One Toke"

"You're alright..." he complimented me, smacking me on the back, as we walked back down the stairs.

When we got to the job site, Willie handed me a pair of black rubber boots that fit over my street shoes. We both put on our boots along side a big booth, with freshly installed and painted walls and doors. GCU was re-purposing the room for who knows what.

"What are we doing now, Willie?" I asked as we entered the big echoey room.

"Strippin'", he answered.

Hey man, I'll take a reluctant hit off your joint, but I'm not taking my clothes off for you, no matter what the boss says.

But looking around at the floor machine and 5 gallon cans of floor stripper, I realized we would be stripping the old epoxy finish off the concrete floor.

"You can wear one of those if you want, but I'm not going to..." Willie said, pointing at a couple respirators. I fitted mine to my face.

Willie opened a can of the stripper, and poured it out on the floor. Handing me a squeegee on a broomstick, he ordered me to "Spread it around" as he got behind the handlebars of the circular floor stripping machine.

"Keep opening 'em up and spreading it around while I strip"

Breathing deep the noxious fumes ,Willie had a great time slipping and sliding behind this floor scrubbing horsey.

Laughing hysterically as he spun around like a top holding the handle of the machine. Willie was getting higher by the minute, sucking in the floor stripper laced air. I watched his brain cell count drop, like the ball in Times Square on New Years Eve.

Clearly, this guy was insane. But he was having an awfully good time. I enjoyed watching this lunatic as I tried to keep my own footing on the slick floor. This stripper was slicker than snot. And Wille's snot was mostly stripper by the time his ride was over. I kept my respirator firmly in place.

We finished the day vacuuming up the slime. Tomorrow I would be in another place with someone else being their grunt and gofer, on another adventure. But plainly, I was back at Boeing again.

9
MOVING ON UP

As a MUM, I was at the very bottom of the food chain in Facilities. And when I was stationed on an actual construction site, the skilled guys loved to pass along their most mundane, strenuous, or dirty jobs to the likes of me.

I'm not complaining, that's just the way it is when you're the low man on the Totem Pole. Either accept it, or see if you'd rather be flipping burgers at McDonalds.

But after being everybody's "boy" for a while, a guy starts looking around for other opportunities around the nation of Boeing. You start searching for a way to be "Moving on Up".

While I was hard at it, the craftsmen I relieved took their well deserved breathers. The production workers in the shops surrounding our construction site were constantly "under the gun", with their work area's being constantly patrolled by supervision.

Eyes would always be peering over to our site to make sure the GCU crew was keeping busy. But as we had done with brooms in my early days, the construction guys knew how to appear busy during their mid shift impromptu breaks.

One trick was to hold your "BS" session while leaning over the tables where the blueprints were sprawled out. Glancing down at the plans, or pointing at some details on the blueprint, created the illusion you were brainstorming on some complex construction issue.

Little did the spies know you were just sharing jokes, or talking about last night's football game.

Our bosses had once held the same jobs themselves, so they all knew the drill. None of them minded standing around shooting the breeze with their guys, as long as slow but steady progress was taking place.

So talking to the boss was another way to make screwing off look like "official business". As long as there were maintenance utility men around to pick up the slack, enough work was being accomplished to appease the headhunters.

There was a clear chain of command. Starting at my lowly position, I was subservient to whoever I was assigned to. Most of them were pretty cool, but others enjoyed the power of being able to push someone around.

Next was the lead-man. Some of them would dig right in and help whenever they could. Others would simply be a presence, there to assign work, and get your parts or supplies, while you continued working.

While of course, we would have welcomed the diversion of being able to walk to the tool room to get our stuff. But the leads kept us in the showroom windows, as living mannequins of the hard working construction men.

The supervisors were substantially higher on the hierarchy, and in those days they wore both clout, and power. They could "can" you on the spot, or be your greatest advocate. As with leads, they had once stood where we were, so they themselves knew every trick in the book. It would behoove anyone to be on their manager's good side.

Above your first line supervisor, were the General Supervisors, Superintendents, and other suits that you didn't want to know, or want them to know you very well either. The ground shook, when they walked the factory floors.

They all were capable of breathing fire, and contrary to popular belief, maybe they DIDN'T put their pants on one leg at a time.

I think the Superintendents used Maintenance Utility Men, as their special butlers to pull their britches up on both legs at once, as they reclined on their management sofas. I was spared from that demeaning duty, as I jack-hammered away for some lowly millwright.

So, as the MUMs, we were the Rodney Dangerfields of the construction crew. We got NO respect. I longed for the good old days on the Maintenance side of Facilities, roaming around the plant. Working at our own pace.

One of the best examples I remember of this "great divide" between the "pawns" and the "kings" of the factory, happened on another floor stripping job at Kent Space Center.

We were preparing the concrete for floor tile on a balcony above a transportation aisle. There were no walls blocking it from the aisle below, but instead a railing at the edge of this floor.

Anticipating that some of this caustic stripper would be sloshing over the edges, we first put barricades, "crime scene tape", cones, and signs all over the aisle to warn people from entering the area.

> *"Floor stripping overhead, Do NOT ENTER"*
> *"Danger STAY OUT"*
> *"Watch out for falling shit on your head"*
> *"No Admittance"*
> *"You'll be SORRY...."*

How many ways could we put it? Surely, anyone with any brains would see the signage. And even hear the commotion taking place above from our noisy machines and stay clear. But the biggest company brains, were sometimes too big for their little britches.

Space Center director, Bill S., might have been smarter than anyone else. But as the Emperor of the Space Center, he wasn't going to be told what to do by anyone. Especially, by impersonal signs. Surely, those warnings didn't apply to anyone as important as he was...he figured.

Stepping over the warning tape, he continued down the aisle engaged in conversation with another VIP as the ocean of floor stripper, sloshed onto the closed beach below us.

He may have been exempt from our warnings by his lofty position, but his halo didn't protect him from the indiscriminate splash of our floor stripper dripping down below.

Glancing over the railing, we saw him wiping the irritating slime off of his bald head. He had been MOSTLY bald before his stroll through the acid rain, but I think we eliminated his few remaining follicles.

His face was red as he looked up angrily to our dutiful crew, scrubbing away like good little MUMs. I couldn't tell if it was the red face of rage, or from chemical burns, but we had done all that we could to prevent his misfortune.

Later, this same Bill S. was implementing some novel new philosophies, that would revolutionize the Boeing work culture. Competition from Japanese manufacturers was giving Detroit a run for their money, Boeing was becoming very interested in learning the secrets of the success of the Toyotas and Hondas.

New approaches to our processes were being introduced daily. Borrowing from the Japanese paradigm, our warehouses for parts were being sold in favor of "just in time" deliveries.

Our comfortable, but cluttered shop area's were being organized by the Five "S" program of Sort, Simplify, Standardize, Sweep, and Self

Discipline. Gone were the days of having anything you needed for your job, found in a heap, within a 10 foot circle of your job.

In Facilities, it meant cleaning up the areas, and labeling everything. So that everyone would know that a galvanized garbage can, was a garbage can. If you read the labels. I'm sure Bill didn't think the labels applied to him, so a MUM would probably have to gather his trash, and put in in the can for him.

In the wake of these changes, there would be less time spent on the job sites for most of us, and more hours spent in conference rooms as the employees were summoned into committees.

There were many other changes coming to the Lazy B, that I will get to along the way. Overall, the changes would come to be known as "Lean Manufacturing" A real culture shock, for fat MUMs like myself.

I was about to be taken far away from where all this political and cultural upheaval was taking place. Dan, my boss, asked me if I'd be willing to help out by going on second shift for a couple of weeks.

The manufacturing calendar is different from the one used by the rest of the world. And I found out that a "couple of weeks" in Boeing time, means over 30 years. I never saw the light of day shift again, for the rest of my career.

Not that I minded. I'd always been a "night owl" anyway, and the pay was better with a 50 cent, and later a 75 cent an hour pay differential for working swing shift.

Traffic on the commutes was much better on second and third shift. Plus, away from all the uptight, bitter, sleep deprived managers and workers on day shift, work life is happier and more relaxed, on the off shifts.

Working with the crafts on second shift, I was fortunate to learn a good many skills. I learned how to layout forms, pour, and finish concrete.

I also learned how to work with plastic, copper, and steel pipe. How to fabricate steel sliding shop doors from scratch, cutting the iron frames, forming sheet metal, and riveting it all together. I even learned how to lay, mud and tape sheetrock from good old, Stormin' Norman, the kindly old carpenter.

But on second shift, I finally started moving. Not moving UP, yet. Along with a few other new hire Maintenance Utility Men, I found myself hucking furniture on the "Move Crew"

Myself, another Irish kid named Mike, and Ernest, a recently discharged Army guy, whom I called "Sarge", a happy go lucky Millwright named Gary, and our lead man, John "W", made up our crew.

We were "second string" to the established, well entrenched existing move crew, led by their supervisor, Glen.

I had met Glen once before, on overtime when I was still on day shift.

My boss Dan, had asked me to stay over, to start sweeping up on a room that GCU had just remodeled. While waiting for Glen to come by with his instructions.

Wanting to make a good impression, I was sweeping like a professional janitor, when this guy who looked almost exactly like Captain Kangaroo walked in the door.

He said nothing, but just stood there staring at me with contempt, as I continued to sweep.

"Get over HERE..." were the first words out of his mouth.

I didn't appreciate his tone, so I shifted on down to low gear, and took my time carefully leaning my broom up against the wall. I strolled slowly over to the door to greet this ornery children's TV show host lookalike.

"Yeah?" I said expressionless, obviously UN-thrilled to meet this supervisor.

"You must be Sweeney...I've heard that you're pretty good"

I nodded.

"We'll see about that..." he said skeptically.

Nice to meet you too, I thought. Although he never introduced himself, it didn't take a genius to figure out the captain was Glen. I wish Captain Kangaroo had sent Mr Green Jeans to meet me instead.

I followed Glen off to take care of some demeaning grunt work that was beneath insulting his skilled workers with

But when we joined the move crew, they called us, the "B" team while we were still under the command of Dan. Glen's boys, were the "A" team. I'll bet that you can guess who got the "gravy" moves, and who got the shit jobs.

The "A" team was led by a guy who looked like a "Cowboy", named Rick. He wore the boots and hat, and looked and sounded, like he was still out riding on the range.

Tommy was a fat kid who looked a lot like Chris Farley, from Saturday Night Live, who had played "Tommy Boy" in the movie. John S, was a lanky, fidgety guy with long hair. Jim looked like a frat boy.
These guys didn't care much for the "B" team. And we weren't too crazy about them either.

For both teams, the work was either feast or famine. When we had moves, we would roll up our sleeves and bust our tails to get things done. When there was no work, we were authorized to do whatever we wanted, so long as we kept out of sight.

Through the teamwork, we all became pretty good friends on the "B" team. Gary, was our entertainment coordinator, and he would always supply the crew with new card and board games to keep us busy in the slow times.

Mike was hilarious. He was a quick wit, and would always save his best routines for me, when I had a mouthful of Coke.

His favorite sight was to watch my dual faucets turn on, as the soda sprayed out of my nostrils, cued by his crazy jokes. We had a lot of fun, but we really got the work done too.

After work, Mike, Sarge, and I, sometimes Gary too would stop off at the Blinker tavern, to shoot pool and drink beer.

Mike was very outspoken and brash, and he almost got into a fight at the bar one night. We were a real crew, looking out for each other. So if it had come to it, we all would have had to jump in with our fists.

Eventually they merged our two move crews into one, and even though we learned to get along and accept each other, there would always be two separate factions within our crew. We would forever be, the "B" team.

The move crew is when I first met our Teamster "Limo" driver Kenny, who would drive us to the furniture moves at the other plants.

The "limo" wasn't a Lincoln Continental. Limo was just an expression. They were vans, that Boeing used to transport the big shots, and the little shots like us around. Kenny had a clever trick to get around in traffic, when he was driving alone.

He had "borrowed" 'Resuscitation Annie', the CPR training doll from the first aid classes. Propping her up in the passenger seat, Kenny was able to travel in the carpool lanes, every time, anytime.

Not only did he have his occupant in the seat, but cops would probably even let him cheese a little on the speed limit. With her pale skin, open mouth and dazed eyes, Annie didn't look so good. They probably figured they were on the way to the hospital.

Kenny took us to a move at "R.B.", the Renton Benaroya plant, where I smashed in my first and only Boeing wall. I would "take care" of a couple of Boeing doors later with my forklift, but I only bashed through one wall in my career.

The site's maintenance supervisor, Monte, had asked me to move a pallet down a narrow hallway, using a stand on "stacker", with a little steering wheel. GCU had just finished up their project, and they were cleaning up the spoils of their construction.

These stackers took a little practice and getting used to because of the odd way that they steered.

Someone started walking toward me in the opposite direction, assuming that I was a professional at driving this contraption. I wasn't.

As a first timer, I panicked, and trying to avoid, smearing the pedestrian all over the clean, new floor, I instead bashed the pallet right through the wall. With Monte and a whole bunch of facilities guys standing only feet away, watching my demolition, shocked, but amused. The paint on the wall wasn't even dry yet.

I thought I was going to be in big trouble, but Monte just laughed, and asked his carpenters and painters to fix my carnage.

Still, as I set my sights on bigger and better things than the move crew, I fancied myself as becoming a forklift driver someday. Driving around picking stuff up without even getting out of your seat, sounded like a great way to make a living.

The off-site "field trip" moves were my favorites. On second shift, with all the VIPS gone home for the day, lunches on the road, lasted as long as it took us to eat. And until we had a chance to let our food digest. As long as we would be able to finish our work, that is. We always made sure we got 'er done. But our half hour lunch breaks could stretch for hours.

Some of those lunches were mostly liquid diets too. I recall one lunch at the Spot tavern, where we lost track of how many pitchers of beer we had killed, before returning to "stagger" the desks and file cabinets, into our "move in place"

Every now and then, Glen, or even our General would make a surprise appearance on one of our off-site moves.

"Where have you guys been?" they would demand.

"Ahh... we got a late start on lunch" the lead would explain, turning his head away to avoid sharing his beer breath with the boss.

"Where's Sweeney....? I need to talk to him..."

"Ummm, I think he's in one of the cans...."

Warned that the boss was on the warpath, I'd suddenly have to "go", in the worst way. In fact, I'd be spending the rest of the night hidden away in the stall of one of the many bathrooms.

The boss must have figured that I wasn't feeling very well. But after six or eight beers, I was actually feeling exceptionally well. Other than a case of the Rainer flu...

We played hard, but we worked hard too. Wrestling 12 foot solid wood conference tables up 3 flights of a windy staircase. Moving hundred of totes, desks, files and safes.

Once we did a 16 hour move, humping hard all night. We kind of earned our easy times, I figured. We kept in pretty good shape, and we were all proud that no matter how big the job, we could gang up on it and get it done as good as anyone could.

One time, in the hustle to get things moving, I picked up a heavy iron safe dolly from the back of a pickup truck, and slammed it down hard on my big toe instead of the concrete.

The mandatory steel toe shoes would have come in handy that day. But the dolly didn't just bounce off the rubber toes of my sneakers. I was like hitting my toe with a sledge hammer.

The howls of my suffering echoed all around the plant.

I set a new world's record for hopping around on one foot for the next 5 minutes. Cursing the dolly, and cursing myself for being so careless. I wouldn't soon forget about this incident.

As I tried to sleep that night, with every beat of my heart, my toe would painfully pulse, reminding me, "Hey Dummy....Remember when you dropped that safe dolly on my face?"

"Oh yeah....I sure do", I replied silently, yawning. I'd remember even after my toenail turned black, and eventually fell off. But reporting it would have added insult to my injury. I would have been written up for not wearing safety shoes, and also ruin the safety record for my crew.

Although a lot of guys got banged up pretty good, reporting your injuries would piss everyone off. As crews, we loved to get a steady flow of gifts for working so safely.

Boeing kept us well supplied with jackets, thermoses, sleeping bags, flashlights, and other cool presents for making safety our number one job. We were often seen limping out with armfuls of safety rewards in our good arm. Or with the slings we wore on our bad arms we had injured on the job, packed full of gifts.

A few years later, I sliced my thumb open on some metal "banding" material. A river of blood trailed behind me as I went looking for some paper towel to bandage up the gouge.

"You need to get that looked at..." The female janitorial lead insisted, as she noticed me ready to bleed out. "Why don't you mind your own business", I thought, as the blood began to pool at my feet.

"No, it's okay...I'll just wrap it up. Thanks", I answered, waving her off, with my dripping, mangled, blood red hand.

"If you don't report it, then I WILL" she declared. Soon I was sitting beside Resuscitation Annie in Kenny's limo on my way to Valley General Hospital.

Kenny and the lifeless heart attack lady, waited in the van, while the doctor sewed my thumb back together with 12 stitches.

After I'd ruined our safety record, of course I was shunned by my friends for a couple days. Plus, I was awarded the title of "Safety Monitor" by my boss. That'll teach me!

NEXT time I'm mortally wounded, I'll just find a dark corner to go off in, and die. So that the crew can keep those hats, and sleeping bags rolling in,

I met my wife, Karen at the Plaza of Kent Space Center. I know, the "Plaza" sounds like some ritzy hotel, but that's not what it was.

The Plaza's were the not so ritzy, little cafes around the plant, where they would reheat and recycle the cafeteria's leftovers. And serve them to us after the main dining area's were closed. Karen was the lunch lady.

I kept her busy, as I would fill my soup bowl up to the brim, and leave a trail to my seat with the soup that would slop out of my bowl. She looked cute, swinging that mop after my every meal. After more than 30 years, she's still cleaning up my messes. Thanks honey!

Although the "B" team was never his favorite, eventually Glen came to accept us, like stepchildren to his beloved "A" team brood. But there was no love lost when Glen transferred out, and we got our new, much feared leader, Cliff "B".

His reputation was abominable. Cliff's nickname was the "executioner". and hearing he was to be our boss, we all feared for our jobs.

Cliff was smug and sarcastic, and he gloried in his dark image. He knew of his hangman acclaim, and loved the cautious respect that it earned him from his underlings. He too, dressed like someone in the Mafia, and his demeanor was distinctly, Robert De Niro.

But it didn't take me long to see through his charade. Cliff was a pussycat really, as long as he was convinced that you feared and respected him.

He would joke and tease the guys, and over time we learned we could dish SOME of it back it him, as long as we acknowledged the limits. And that we acted like we knew that he had our lives in his hands.

More importantly, he showed no favoritism. To him, us "B" team-ers were just as subject to his abuse as the "A" Team was. When our lead went on vacation, he even granted me a temporary grade 8 lead position, just because I had the guts to be the first to suggest it to him.

Some of our moves were lucrative too. For instance, when an office bay was going to be carpeted, we would move the furniture and totes out into a hallway on a Friday night.

The carpet crew would install the rug on Saturday, so we would get the time and a half day off. Then return for overtime on the double time Sunday, and have the office all set up for the workers on their Monday morning arrival.

So we'd skip the measly time and a half pay, and have half of a weekend to enjoy. And still get the big pay. It was a sweet deal.

But it was feast or famine, and Cliff knew as well as Glen had, that there was times when his movers had little to do. He was content with us hiding out, lying low during those well earned reprieves.

The janitorial crews didn't have such luxuries however, and their bitter supervisors, a female named "Butch" and an ex-painter named Dave would frequently catch us and snitch to Cliff.

Confronted with this accusation, Cliff would have to reprimand us, to save his own face.

The irony is that I knew Dave when he was a painter lead, and he was the company's biggest joker, clown, and screw off. The management necktie he wore, sure squeezed a lot of self righteousness into his hypocritical, big mouth.

Honestly, the crew all laughed when Dave and Cliff had snuck off to attend a Seahawks game one evening. And the network TV cameras captured them quickly trying to conceal their faces as they zoomed in.

The commentators also laughed, remarking, "It appears somebody's not supposed to be here tonight..." The cameras lingered on them, and pursued them mercilessly, as all of America laughed at the bad boys.

Their big boss happened to be watching the game at home on his sofa, and he wanted autographs from the naughty supervisors the next day. On corrective action memos. I did feel bad for Cliff, but I shed no tears for Dave when the teeth of karma had finally bitten him on his smart ass.

Overall, the move crew was great fun, and as time passed, even the A and B crews became less segregated. A bunch of us even jumped out of an airplane together. But I had my sights set on bigger and better things. I still envied the lifestyle of those free spirited forklift drivers.

On some of our moves, there were sit down electric stackers, that were exactly like little forklifts. We would use these to bring pallets out to the forklift drivers. I would always be the first to run to the driver's seat, and take on that responsibility.

I made it well known to Al, the forklift supervisor, that I had been grooming myself for the forklift job on those stackers. And that I would appreciate being considered for the next opening for an M.E.O.

Position (MEO means Motive Equipment Operator, aka Forklift, or "Jitney" Driver)

10
A LIFTER'S LIFE

Al was a great boss. A friendly, decent, stand up guy.

He looked a little like Jiminy Cricket, and Al carried that same wise, cheerful, spirit that Pinocchio's friend exhibited.

I hated "glad handing" him with my forklift aspirations, because it probably made me look like I was just "sucking up", to get the job. I wasn't, but if hanging around with Al DID get me behind the wheel of a forklift, I wasn't going to turn it down.

Al respected the fact that I was trying to better and advance myself, and sure enough, soon I was a officially a forklift driver. But initially, most of my lifting was done with my hands, rather than with my jitney.

As the new kid on the block, I was assigned to "Xerox Paper Duty" Instead of driving a real forklift, I used a ride on stacker, just like the one that I had driven as a mover, to load pallets of paper on my flatbed truck. From the truck, I would hand deliver to all of the copy machines around the Kent Space Center plant with a dolly.

It was a perfect job for me, actually. I was basically on my own, running at my own pace. The transportation canopy had always been like the Berlin wall, with stacked pallets of paper sky high. The supply

99

never waned much. I challenged myself to get it all delivered, and finally eliminate those walls.

Lifting tons of the 40 pound boxes each day, kept me in great shape. Traveling far and near, with my push cart loaded to capacity, I would restack the paper by the copy machines.

No one had ever done it before, but I had tamed the paper monster under the canopy. From then on, after taking care of the fresh supply that came in, I earned my breaks for the rest of the day.

But many times, I would volunteer my services to our grade 8 forklift lead, Fred, rather than just taking it easy. Fred had been a driver for many years, and I figured there was much that I could learn from him.

As an older guy, trying to ease into his upcoming retirement in a few years, Fred was tickled that he could pawn off a little more of his work off to someone else.

Fred had done his time in the Marines, and as an MEO. He had now decided that his skills should be specialized. He would offload the flatbed semi trailers that came into the yard, but leave all of the deliveries to the "B" men.

The extent of the "training" Fred gave me was, "Take those pallets over to the 18-62 building"

"Anything I should know Fred, any tips...?" I asked

"Yes. Keep your forks low to the ground"

I stabbed my first pallet, and took off on my first official delivery. I had worked in Kent Space Center for a couple years by now. So I knew that the roll up door behind those dirty strips that USED to be transparent, was ALWAYS left open. ALWAYS.

I couldn't see if anyone was on the other side of those grimy drive through strips, I slowly crept through them, and honked my horn to warn pedestrians to get out of the way. I'd seen the other drivers do the same.

The sound of my horn covered up the sound of my forks knocking the bottom edge of the steel roll up door right it's tracks. I did feel a little resistance as I pushed the pedal. So I backed off. I guess those doors were not ALWAYS left open, after all.

Beginners luck I guess. I felt like my career was over before I even got started. Picking up my radio, I made the call to dispatch.

"Can you have Al meet me at door S-4 of the 62 building?"

"Ten four"- Shirley, the voice of dispatch replied.

Before Al could arrive, I thought I'd try something. I rolled the wounded door up part way, and drove my forklift around to the other side of it. Carefully pushing with my forks, I flexed the bottom edge back the other way, and popped the door back in place on it's tracks.

When Al arrived, other than a couple insignificant scratches, and tiny fork dents, it was as good as new. Or, at least as good as the old well beaten door was before I had impaled it.

Good old Al was sympathetic, and just advised me to go slow, check things out first, and to be more careful No disciplinary action was warranted.

Back at the Canopy, Fred gave me a tip.

"When something like that happens, don't go telling the boss right away. Let me take a look at it first."

"Okay Fred" I agreed. He was the lead. If that's what he tells me to do, then that's what I'll do.

"Hey kid....Don't take it so hard. We all break things now and then, it goes with the job...." Fred added.

"Thanks Fred"

I'd do my fair share of breaking things in my time as an MEO. My next hit came a couple of weeks later, when I ran my fork through an actual production part.

Fred can't fix this, I thought. I'm screwed. But amazingly, Fred had a simple solution. He picked up the small, damaged part, and tossed it over the fence outside the property. My mouth popped open, and my eyes bugged out at the sight.

"We can't do that, can we?" I asked with disbelief.

"We didn't. I did. And you didn't see anything, DID you?", the Marine asked.

."But, what if...?" I began. Fred didn't hear me. He was already driving back to the canopy.

He had changed the whole dynamic of the problem. I was willing to own up to my mistake, and face the music, regardless of the consequences. But I wasn't a snitch, and to report it now, would have meant throwing well meaning Fred, under the bus. So, I just let it go. Sorry Boeing.

In addition to Fred only working the transportation canopy, on Monday nights in the fall, Fred was done for the night by 7:00 pm.

"Hey, it's Monday night football. You young guys can take care of everything. I'm watching the game"

We "B" drivers weren't allowed in his special "crib". Fred and all the "A" men from all the crafts were huddled together in teleconference with Don Meredith and Howard Cosell. Rooting for their favorite teams, while we "B" drivers were left holding down the fort.

So Fred was madder than a sacked quarterback, when I came in one night, and told him that I had dropped a dumpster in the "hugehaul", while I was dumping garbage.

Fred didn't participate in the rescue, but he stood by and instructed me, as I rummaged through the garbage, rigging the big dumpster with chains, so I could hoist it out with my forks. Yelling commands at me, with an ugly, "I'm missing my game" scowl on his face.

He knew the procedure well. I'm pretty sure he must have dropped one or two dumpsters in the hugehaul himself, sometime in his long, illustrious fork lifting career.

Over time, I got to be pretty good on the machine. The forks became like an extension of my own hands, and I could manipulate almost anything to go where I wanted it. Either by picking up, or bumping and pushing with my forks in just the right spot.

I also became an ace at backing up all kinds of trailers. Oddly, these days, when I try to back up my own little utility trailer with my car, I know absolutely nothing about it anymore.

Driving forklift, was everything that I had imagined. There was a freedom and a joy in coming to work, that cannot be found when someone is lashed to a desk or fenced into a work area. I had truly found my niche, that fit snugly with my skills, and my disposition.

Fred felt he had earned his "King of the Hill" position. So, on cold days he would delegate even more of his tasks to us. "I like to wrap up in a nice warm building" was one of his trademark sayings, as he would send us out into the Seattle winter's cold and rain.

I couldn't complain. I was making good money, keeping busy, and loving it. Although our forklifts had no roofs or windows at the time, they had a great flow of warm air from the radiator blowby, and exhaust to dry our drenched clothes. As we shivered in the rain, rubbing our hands together in the blast.

Remember Dave? That busybody painter/supervisor who used to squeal on the move crew until he got nailed for being AWOL at the Seahawks game?

Well, Mr Buttinski followed me into the forklifts with his annoying, "making my business his business", ways.

I walked into the supervision office for something, and Dave noticed my shoes.

"Nice shoes", he remarked sarcastically, pointing at my sneakers. "Hey Al", he called to a desk a few feet away, "Aren't your boys supposed to be wearing steel toed shoes?"

I might have felt differently if Dave had been honestly concerned about my safety. But he was just in his zone, making trouble for the sake of making trouble. That's how he got his jollies.

Al never would have made a fuss about my footwear, but Dave had pushed him into a corner. "Ed, we're really are supposed to be wearing safety shoes..."

"I know Al, but they just kill my feet. I'll be careful..." I pleaded for an exemption.

"I'm sorry Ed, but I'm going to have to insist that you either wear steel toes, or else wear 'clompers'"

Clompers, were the stupid looking, tool room issue, yellow toe caps that you would strap around your ankles. They made you sound like you were a horse walking around on the concrete floors. I hated them.

But I had to march around like "Flicka" for a couple of weeks, until everybody forgot about my steel toe warning. "Thanks Dave...You happy now?" I scoffed.

Al was a great boss, and I hated it when he was transferred. But fortunately, my next supervisor was also a great guy who put the interests of his workers at the top of his agenda. Steve and Al, were both a couple of the all time greats in Boeing management.

As I transitioned from being a mover, to a paper delivery boy, to a sit down driver, I started to lose some of my fitness. And gain some of my fat back. And adding to the sedentary nature of my job, I was appointed leader of our improvement team, which set me in a chair even longer.

We were pioneering "Self managing Crews", where the supervisors were just there as advisers, and the forklift crews were to manage their own affairs. Our work on second shift began to pile up as the day-shift committees spent most of their days in conference with one another.

That was all fine and well. If the company wanted it that way, we would pick up the slack as all the day shift Forklift "executives" abandoned their jitneys in favor of their bureaucratic duties. Until, they sent a nasty memo about their intentions to "incite controls" over the other shifts.

I wrote a scathing rebuttal memo, and soon was in a face to face meeting with my leader counter parts from first shift along with the General Supervisors.

I slammed the offending memo on the conference table, and swore at their supreme leader, Big Jim, calling him by a very insulting "fighting word" name.

Jim rose up from the table, his fists clenched, and I probably came pretty close to getting an early start on getting my set of dentures. But our supervision intervened with a call for "calm heads".

We tried to iron things out, but left with a pretty wrinkly relationship between our shifts. Later, as Jim complained to our General Supervisor Ron about some alleged deficiency from second shift on his master plan, Ron said, "Don't tell me. Ed is the second shift leader. Tell him..."

"I can't" Jim explained. "I never see him at shift change. He's always running to punch in, as we're walking out...."

I always had had my own interpretation of what being "on time" meant. Some say, that it means "being in your work area, ready to go". But to me, on time meant just being on the premises, and or punched in (if required, in this case it wasn't) as the bell rang.

Boeing was placing a great emphasis on "just in time" inventory at that time. I was just extending the principle to include attendance, as well as inventory.

Ron confronted my boss Steve about this. "Is it true...?" he asked

Steve acknowledged, but he praised my work, and my efforts on the self management program.

"Well, you need to write him up" Ron ordered.

"I'm not going to write him up, he's one of my best guys" Steve said

"Then I'll write YOU up..." Ron responded to Steve's insubordination.

"Fine...do it!", Steve replied as he walked away.

Ron backed down, and I never got written up, neither did Steve. But I awarded my boss with tons of respect for his loyalty to his guys.

When a boss is an advocate for his crew, that crew will do anything to help that boss. It does eventually come back in the companies favor, when management joins in with the comradeship of it's workers, I believe.
Another example of a great boss rolling up his sleeves on behalf of his boys, came a couple years later, at PSD. I had brought in a small TV for us to watch during our breaks, lunches, and slow times in the forklift/crane break-room.

A shop supervisor who didn't care much for one of our crane operators, Tony, came in during break one day and told Tony to shut off the TV. "You're not even supposed to have a TV in here" he sneered.

"I'm not going to shut it off...It's not mine, and I didn't turn it on", Tony retorted.

"Okay, smart guy...Let's just see what your boss has to say about this"

He called our new boss, Mike to come over from nearby Kent Benaroya to discuss this. Mike was formerly a crane operator, and he understood the cyclic nature of our work.

"Is the work getting done?" Mike asked.

"Yes, but that's not the point..." the shop boss argued.

"No, that IS the point..." Mike emphasized.

"Well, I'll have to talk to YOUR boss" the shop supervisor snapped back.

"Talk to anybody you want. If the works getting done, then you go manage your guys, and I'll manage mine!" Mike finished the discussion, walking away.

The debacle ended uneventfully. But just to be on the safe side, I took my TV home that night.

Again, I emphasize, bosses like Mike and Steve never had to worry about getting support when they were in a bind. When managers treated their guys right, everyone's back was watched. And the company scored.

But Mike came later. I was still a greenhorn driver at Kent Space Center.

Just when I couldn't have been happier working at my job, another wave of surplussing hit. And I found myself being washed over to the Robbins Site. But before we go over there, let's stop off and get a drink.

11
WATERING HOLES AND FISHING HOLES

The hourly guys, were the workhorses of Boeing. And like a good team of horses, we would gather at our favorite feeding troughs, and the watering bins as a team.

The Annex Tavern near Boeing Field, the Spot, the Blinker, and the Pony Keg Taverns in the Kent Valley, Soft Sams, and the Dog and Pony in Renton were where the Boys filled their tanks, and let off steam.

"Rack 'em up", was often heard at the pool table, as the sound of pitchers of beer were been poured from a keg, like a soothing creek. You could taste the butter in the air from the popcorn machines.

Conversation would start softly, and civilly, then crescendo as the beer loosened our inhibitions. I think it says something about Boeing and the love we all felt for our favorite airplane company, that the talk was mostly "shop talk".

Small talk, about what we had done earlier in the day, would evolve into big talk about how much more we did than the other guys, after a couple schooners. Bragging about our gifts of labor we'd given to the company, would change into bitching about some crazy new policy, or our new boss or General, as we reached the bottom of another pitcher.

We might talk a little about sports or something in the news, but Boeing was the common thread that kept us together, on and off the job.

After our words began to slur a bit, somebody might say, "Hey...we ought to all go fishin'...." The next day, someone would have already contacted a charter boat, and was organizing the event, taking down names.

I once started a "Hey guys...Let's go SKYDIVING" campaign, after pounding down a few at the Blinker.

A couple of guys on the move crew jumped right on board. "I'm in...." Mike volunteered, "Let's do it" said Rick.

Ernest, was a little more hesitant. "I don't know...Why would I want to jump out of a perfectly good airplane....?"

I could have said, "Because it's there", or "Come on...You only go around once". But instead, I chose the "Come on....You CHICKEN!" challenge. Unfortunately, it worked.

Truthfully, I had always planned to someday jump from one of those single engine planes up at Issaquah. But "someday", is usually a an abstract future date, that hardly ever arrives.

Once you start throwing the "C" word (for "chicken") around , you had better be willing to take the plunge yourself. And when you "razz" the other guys to show that they've got a pair, you're expected to be at the front of the line, to go through with it. But whether intoxicated or sober, I really was up for the challenge that I had made.

"Sure I'll jump, it will be fun" I'd always said. UNTIL, the dream, that is.

After I had already stirred up the guys, and gotten them all fired up to take the "Geronimo" leap , I had a terrifying nightmare. It was one of those "falling" dreams, where you wake up in a cold sweat, trembling.

My dream seemed even more real than my reality did. And I thought, "This is a real BAD omen. I'd have to be crazy to jump after this dream"...

But as most young men, I couldn't back down after my braggadocio coaxing of Ernest to "be a man" and jump with us. My "manhood" was on the line.

For the weeks leading up to our jump, I felt as though my days were numbered. My dream seemed to be almost a prophetic warning. But, it I would have weaseled out of it, I would never live it down. I HAD to jump.

On the eve of my sky "dying" jump, as I figured it was going to be, I went off by myself to one of those watering holes. To fill my gut with a good dose of liquid courage. And to forget about the danger, just loosen up and be happy on this, my "last night".

I don't know how I ever got home, but early that next morning, I was not so happy. Instead, I had an epic hangover.

I drove out to the jumping site, praying, with a throbbing head. "I probably won't have much chance to say it later...But forgive me for all the stuff I've done" I asked before I got to the airport for my final, busy day.

First off, there was ground school for four hours. I tried to pay attention, but it wasn't easy when I was hungover, tired, and feeling doomed. I did catch the "highlights" of the training, and they weren't comforting.

"Here we are", the jump master said, squeaking chalk on the blackboard. "And here is the Freeway" Which ran right next door to the jump school. "If you land there, you're dead"
Then he drew a circle. "This is Lake Sammamish. If you land in there, you're dead. Your chute will drag you under the water, and you'll drown".

He pointed through the window, looking outside. "You see those power lines? If you land in them, you're dead. They will fry you"

"If your main chute doesn't open, you have to cut it away...otherwise it will get tangled up with the reserve chute and you're dead" I thought, "Is that all?"

"That's not all", he answered my unspoken question, "I want you to keep your hand covering over the reserve chute at all times while in the plane. Because if your "pilot chute" starts to deploy inside the plane, it can get caught up, catch wind, and take the whole airplane down. So, If that happens, I'm throwing you out" And then I'll die.

So, I took in all the horrible ways that I might meet my maker, but somehow I missed the part about making sure that your helmet is strapped down, good.

We all suited up, and did some practice "landings" from a little platform. Then we were packed into the tiny plane like sardines. I was sweating so bad. as I took in what I figured were to be my last few minutes of air, that it probably smelled a little like sardines too. Rick was the first to jump to the relief of the fresh air.

When he let go of the strut, I heard a startling slap, on the side of the plane. I thought it sounded like "breaking bones" A quiver went up my spine.

"That's just the static line hitting the fuselage", the jump master explained. He looked at me and shouted, "Get out there and hang"

At least in Issaquah, you didn't just leap out into the open air. First, you sat on the entry door threshold, Then, on command, you'd have to grab the strut that holds the wings, and hang, until the jump master tells you to let go.

Up until that point, I could have been a wimp, and said, "Look, I changed my mind, thanks for the ride" But once I grabbed the strut, my terror turned into laughter.

Not that I was any less sure that "this was it" for me... It's just that once you are hanging, you're at the mercy of the wind, and there was no way that you would ever be able to work your way back into the plane.

The heavy breeze is pushing your legs back like you're Superman. And whether you crash or land safely, you're finding your own way to the ground from that point on. So it doesn't do you any good to cry. You might as well laugh, as you prepare to leave this world. So I did.

When the time was right, he shouted, "Let go". I fell incredibly fast. It was exhilarating, in a terrifying way. As the static line tightened, my parachute opened, and it felt like a "bungee cord" slowly putting the brakes on my quick fall.

My helmet rose up, and was sitting like a crown on the top of my head, wedged in place by the lines of the parachute rising up from my harness.

"Oh yeah, now I remember, I was supposed to buckle it down...." I tried to fumble around with the helmet, but I was mostly trying to see if I had a good chute, or "canopy" as we'd learned to call them, above me. First things first.

The next thing I knew, I was floating 2800 feet above the ground, watching my helmet plummet toward the ground at terminal velocity. The ride down after the free fall ended had a nice view, but it wasn't really scary.

It was more like being on a Ferris Wheel, just a very high up one. I managed to avoid the freeway, the lake and the power lines, and landed uneventfully and softly, on my butt.

At the conclusion, all was well. Except the jump school people were pretty upset about the helmet. But no one died that day, either from skydiving, or from metallic blue helmets falling from the sky.

"I'm ready to go again" Rick said, excitedly. "Me too", said Ernest.

"I'm not going to push my luck", I responded. I had dodged the bullet of my falling dream. Having "been there" and "done that", I don't think that I'll ever jump from any perfectly good airplanes anymore. Or even from bad ones.

But inside the company gates or outside, Boeing workers were like "Frat Brothers" We came together as strangers, and became friends over the years.

Even today, bumping into those that you have worked with, struck with, or jumped from 2800 feet with, it's always like a little class reunion. We were all a part of the history of aviation, and a part of each others lives.

That's the way it works when you come from the colony of "Bees" We sometimes drank together, and often flew together. Once in a while, even fell from the skies together.

But now back on the ground, let's head over to my new assignment at the Robbin's site.

12
BECOMING AIRBORNE

I liked being a forklift driver. I might have happily worked in jitneys for the rest of my career. Cranes always looked a little intimidating to me.

But I was forced into the skies by a boss who was trying to hold me down. Piss me off, and I might end up biting off my own nose, to stick my tongue in your face.

Such was the case when I worked for "Marshmallow" (That's not his REAL name, but it's similar to what it was)

"It won't do you any good to sulk" Marshmallow said as I sat on my forklift staring off into space. "Just dump the garbage and do whatever you're told, and maybe in 15 or 20 years, you can get to be an "A" man"

"Are we DONE here?", I asked.

"Yes" said Marshmallow.

I fired up my rig and drove away. At my first opportunity, I pulled out a pen and paper, and started writing.

Dear Terry (the Facilities General supervisor)

I'd like to be considered for the crane operator position opening up at the Robbin's site. I've spent the last couple of years in material handling, as a fork lift driver, and I think I would be a natural fit for this position.

In the last few months I've been in a unique position to observe the flow of the crane operation. I'm well acquainted with the hardware they handle, and get along well with the shop personnel

I've also been working closely along side the crane operators who will be training me. We work well together and I'm confident I would be a welcome member of the crew, and an asset to the team.

I'm looking forward to starting soon. Thank you for your consideration.

Ed Sweeney

Or something like that. I put it in the in-plant mail. And just to be fair, I put a copy of the letter on Marshmallow's desk too. So he knew what I was up to.

There wasn't a chance in hell that he would have given me the job without hedging my bets by contacting the general. So, I was willing to wait for general Terry's response. I went back to work.

A short time later, Marsh (I've shortened his name for brevity) waved me down as I was making some deliveries of pallets on my forklift.

"Nice letter" he said. "You'll start training on Monday".

I drove away grinning. My letter had forced his hand. Not that I was crazy about becoming a crane operator. But I was livid about being passed over for a short term temporary "A" driver's slot, in favor of a six months of seniority man. He was Marsh's little buddy from K.B. (Kent Benaroya)

For a little perspective, the normal process is when an "A" man goes on vacation, the "B" driver would get to take his spot and pay. But instead, Marsh had taken this man with only 6 months time in the company from KB, given him the job, and sent me over to back fill his position at KB.

If that wasn't enough of a slap in the face, Marsh expected me to spend a few days training this guy, to take my own job away. Understandably I was bitter. So I figured, there's more than one way to skin a cat, and more than one way to get a grade 8 job.

Besides, cranes would be a permanent 8, rather than the temporary fill in position's short term raise.

But did Marsh's decision have merit? I'll let you be the jury. Let's go into the courtroom...

"Did you, Mr Sweeney, run an inlet crate into a roll up door frame, requiring man hours of a millwright to repair?"

"Yes I did"

"And did you damage some asphalt, trying to pick up a pallet on an sloped road surface...?"

"Yes, that happened too"

"No further questions..."

"The prosecution calls Bob, a General Supervisor from Kent Space Center"

"Bob, do you recall Mr Sweeney reporting damage to a one of a kind, graphite ring that was supposed to be going into outer space, had been rolled off a trailer by his forklift?"

"Yes I do"

"No further questions...."

"I wish to cross examine" my attorney says.

"What was your response, Bob?"

"I told Ed, that if nothing ever gets broken, that just means that you're not doing anything...."

"So, you find it excusable that his error might have prevented the launch of this NASA mission?"

"Not excusable, but forgivable. He's an ambitious, hard working HUMAN being. Things happen. Everyone makes mistakes..."

Yes they do. I was living proof of that. And if breaking stuff was the indicator of how hard you're working, I must have been the hardest working forklift driver at Boeing.

But it's true. In a job like forklifts, mishaps do happen. It's part of the learning curve. I guess I was learning a lot! You have to break some eggs to make an omelet. But the omelets I made, had left quite a bit of egg on my face.

On Monday, I had started to train as a crane guy. By Tuesday, I was beginning to have second thoughts about it.

The lifts were all done by remote control, "belly boxes" at the Robbin's site. In other words, we didn't operate them from the air, but with a control box we that we carried with us on the ground. Craning was an exacting job, requiring precise timing, and much attention to detail.

The training was nerve wracking to me. If not for the money, I would have strongly preferred the familiar work of driving a forklift. I wouldn't say that I did well on the cranes, but I did "fair". At the end of the several week training program, despite my best efforts, Marsh gave the job to another, more experienced candidate who had come out of the cranes in Renton.

He told me that I'd done a good job, but that I didn't get the gig. Oh well. I thanked him for the chance, and went happily back to my old job.

For the next month, I was content, going about my daily routine. All I'd wanted was the opportunity, and a fair shake. Given that, I chalked cranes up as an experience to be remembered, and a job to be forgotten.

Then one day Marsh held up the "halt" sign as I was passing by on my forklift.

"The crane job is open again. If you still want it, it's yours", he said.

Marsh had a habit of looking around, and avoiding your face as you spoke to him. If and when he got around to answering you, he took his sweet time. At this point, the crane job vs forklifts was about six of one, a half dozen of the other. So, as he liked to do, I put him on hold for the next minute or two, as I weighed the equation.

Staring off into nowhere, I pondered. The money was far better in cranes. But my job satisfaction was vastly greater on the forklift. Less stress and less money...or more anxiety, and bigger paychecks...?

As the clock ticked away, I wouldn't have been disappointed if Marsh had just left, as I ignored him. But he waited patiently, as everyone always had to do for him.

Finally, I shrugged my shoulders and said, "Yeah, okay. I'll take it...Thanks" And my fate was sealed for the next 26 years. I was a fully fledged crane operator.

13
MAN OVERHEAD

If overhead crane operators were compared to birds flying overhead, then belly box operators were the Penguins and Chickens of the crane kingdom. We spent our time mostly on the ground. Some operators didn't consider radio control to be "real" crane work. It was more like we were playing "video games", to them.

It would be a couple years before I would be flying overhead in the bridge cranes. In the meantime, I was becoming more and more comfortable running the belly boxes at the Robbin's site. And relaxing a bit, I was starting to once again, have a little fun at work.

Boeing is a big user of acronyms, and just to keep us on our toes, they liked to change them around as soon as we got used to them. At the time I started, the Robbin's site housed P. P. and S., which stood for Power Pack and Strut. They soon dropped that abbreviation for P.S.D., which stood for Propulsion Systems Division.

PSD had three functions. The first was to build up the jet engines which came in from the manufacturers as "short blocks". The mechanics would add hydraulic lines, wiring harnesses and duct work to the engines coming in from General Electric, Pratt and Whitney, or Rolls Royce.

121

Secondly, PSD built the struts that attached the engines to the wings.

But, most of the crane work involved the last function at PSD, called the "Fit Check".

We would hang the engines on a "dummy" strut and add the composite cowlings, and thrust reversers to the hanging engine. Mechanics would check their fit, adjust hinges, and make shims as needed. Then we would disassemble the whole package and ship it off to the final assembly plants in Renton or Everett where they would be installed on the airplanes.

Overtime was the norm, not the exception. After what seems like a never ending period of inflated paychecks from the OT, there is a tendency to consider it as your "base pay" and adjust your spending accordingly. At least I did.

It can be a rude awakening when the overtime suddenly stops, and you're wondering how your going to survive on your "real" income. But anyone who has worked for Boeing for decades, realizes that the overtime rug can suddenly be pulled out from under you, when you least expect it.

The Robbin's site was a melting pot of colorful characters.

In fit check, Linn, would be seen hanging from a harness above the strut, swinging and chattering like a monkey as we brought the parts into him with our cranes. He was hardworking. But he relished in his reputation as a lunatic. I think it was just part of his "shtick"

Nearby, Doug and Eric were also fit checking. Both were intelligent, gifted mechanics. Ambitious and driven, they were so much alike, that they couldn't stand one another. I liked them both, but never understood their mutual despise. Maybe it was competitiveness.

On the next strut, Tim was going on about UFOs. He had been hypnotized by his overdose of listening to Art Bell. Obsessed with the alien presence and survival-ism, it was like stepping into a parallel universe to work with Tim. Not that I didn't enjoy visiting his strange planet. Tim was a good guy, for an earthling.

Those idiosyncrasies were balanced out by Bruce and John. Both were pretty much regular ordinary guys, it was a nice break from the monkeys, the fighters, and the extraterrestrials, to just chat about news, sports, or life as we worked with them.

Fit check was ruled by Marty, the lead. He had come from the simple country life in Montana, and the rat race of the big city made his head spin. He was an excellent lead, dedicated to making sure all the work was done properly, and on time. But incredibly nervous about the whole thing.

Jimmy "T" from stores, used to curl Marty's hair. Jimmy was a nice guy, but he got all wound up about everything. His ranting and raving put Marty's "tick" into overdrive. When he was anxious, Marty used to swirl his fingers through the ends of his hair. By the end of the shift, Marty's straight hair looked like he had gotten a perm, thanks to Jimmy.

My crane partners were Tony and Mike. Tony was loud, rambunctious, and very hyper. His energy kind of scared me. When I first met him he was bouncing off the walls, and his loud voice, whether laughing or hollering was startling. Tony was a passionate guy. And he did a lot of both, laughing and hollering.

I wasn't the easiest guy to train, in spite of my eagerness to learn. This crane stuff didn't come very naturally to me. Tony would holler at me when I did something wrong, then he would laugh about it afterwards.

I was trying to quit smoking during my training, and I was nervously and aggressively chewing gum to fight my withdrawals. As well as my anxiety about learning this new craft of craning.

My overly zealous kneading of the gum was driving Tony crazy.

"Take it easy on the chewing..." he hollered, after finishing hollering at me for my latest screw-up on my crane techniques. It was driving him nuts.

"You need to get some cigarettes. If you don't buy a pack, I'll buy one for you" Tony wasn't a smoker, and he hated smoking. But it was better than my constant chomping. Soon, I was lighting up again, like a 100 watt bulb.

Mike J. was an easy going joker, who had been recruited from the steel mills to run crane at Boeing. Everyone liked Mike personally, but they didn't care much for his crane skills.

In the mills, the craning technique they used was called, "bump and run". Quickly picking up loads, swinging down the bays, indifferent to whether they ran into anything or not. No finesse, just pick up a load, get to the destination fast, drop it, and race back for the next lift.

That works fine when you're picking up scrap metal to throw into a melt pot. Not so much with expensive, fragile aircraft parts. Especially moving them in tight quarters with expensive hardware, and fragile fingers of the mechanics working in the pinch points.

Mike was transitioning out of cranes to become the Robbin's site new "A" driver, and I was coming in to back-fill his crane job. The shop personnel hoped that I would turn out to be less scary than Mike.

Mike was the guy who gave me my nickname, "Fast Eddy" Although I was never really that swift, I liked it much better than my previous handle, "Big Ed". I embraced and promoted my new, complimentary moniker.

Mike had a couple of his trademark phrases that he would repeat throughout the day.

"Take a break" he parroted a couple dozen times a day, always with his Bugs Bunny like smile.

Another of Mike's patented slogans was "There's a beer waiting for you in the fridge" There never really was.

But on a hot day I once brought in a "Sharps" near beer, strictly for refreshment, not for intoxication. My boss pointed out, that although it only had a negligible alcohol content, any alcohol at all was in violation of the company rules.

Once, on my way to work, I had picked up a sandwich, soda and chips for lunch at a deli mart along the way. The clerk told me they had run out of bags. So, he offered me an empty box from a half case of Budweiser to use as my lunchbox.

Walking through the gate with the half rack tucked under my right arm, I waved to the gate guard. He waved back, and then did a double take.

"Hey, what have you got there?", he called out to me from 10 yards back.

"Oh this?" I answered. "It's just my LUNCH"

"Come here..." he said, motioning with his finger.

We both laughed when I showed him the contents weren't the liquid lunch he had imagined. But Boeing had really started to clamp down on "contraband" as well as expanding it's definition of "forbidden items"

In my early days with the company, no one said anything about a stack of Playboy or Penthouse magazines sitting on a break room table. "Boys will be boys" was the justification.

But since more and more women had entered the fields that were traditionally held by men, that had changed long ago. As I was becoming a crane operator, the latest target was the "Snap On" calendars and pictures, that were hanging from almost every toolbox.

These were far from pornographic. They just featured attractive women, clad in bikinis. Who smiled, while holding wrenches and screwdrivers. Pretty harmless, if you asked me. But they had recently been declared by the company to be inappropriate for the workplace.

That's all fine and dandy, I guess. But there was a gay guy named Billy, who ironically worked in the "tube shop". And Billy had a big collection of pictures of men posing provocatively in revealing speedos, posted around his work area.

Trying to be all politically correct and accommodating, management looked the other way at Billy's chosen workstation décor. To each their own, and if they hadn't sent the Snap On girls home, I would have endorsed Billy's right to choose his photo albums. But what was good for the geese, didn't apply to the ganders apparently.

Equally disturbing to me was the way management approached a kid who worked in the in-plant mail room, who liked to wear T-Shirts with Christian slogans on them.

"We've had some complaints that your shirts are offending people. I'm going to have to ask that you don't wear them anymore..." his boss told him.

If Boeing had a specified dress code, that would be one thing, But to single him out when they had no qualms about heavy metal Tees with nasty pictures and slogans, I thought he was being unfairly profiled. Had it been me, I think I would have declared discrimination.

Speaking of the mail room, years later I worked in the cranes with Chuckie, who had once been a mail room guy. He told me of some of the contraband that bounced around inside the inner office memo envelopes.

If the mail room staff knew there was candy inside the packages, they were free to indulge. As food was forbidden to be passed through the mail. Anything edible was taboo, especially if it was perishable. One soon to be unemployed hunter, must have been unaware of this rule.

As a joke, this guy had packed up a little venison to send to his friend. When Chuckie's crew noticed blood dripping from the package, they opened it up.

I wouldn't have considered it to be edible, but they were shocked to discover the "meat", was a severed penis from a bull deer. After a hearty, sick laugh, they picked up the phone to call their boss. "Dick...?"

Along with Mike and Tony, we shared our break-room with the janitorial crew. Pearlie, Angie, and Annie, were part of our little work family,

Sometimes work could be a little frustrating for the janitors. Once, coming in for break, Annie who was well past retirement age, threw her rubber gloves on the table, and plopped into her seat, looking disgusted.

I broke out into laughter.

"So, what's so funny", Annie scowled, not in the mood to be laughed at. I pointed to her motionless glove, resting on the table. Everyone including Annie started to bust a gut.

The glove had somehow landed with it's middle finger sticking straight up. It was a perfect editorial cartoon depicting the kind of day she had been having.

As it had been many times before, we became pretty close as a crew, and content with the status quo of our surroundings and colleagues. But as soon as you get comfortable, it must be time for a change, we had all learned by then.

First, Tony was surplussed, and I met Delven who was brought in to replace him. Mike, was also replaced by stodgy, grumpy Ray, as our "A" driver.

Del was a nice guy, but he was the polar opposite of the outspoken, bombastic Tony. I tried to fill Tony's size 14 shoes as the crew's joker, and the talkative one. But I'm only a 10 and a half wide. Things got a little quieter.

Ray wasn't Mike, but you learn to deal with all kinds of personalities in the ever changing world of the Lazy B. Although you might miss the way that things once were, you have no choice but to play the cards you are dealt.

In the next round of card dealing, the Robbin's site was moving to the old B-2 bomber site. It had real overhead cranes, and I was about to become a REAL crane operator. At the Thompson Site, I would finally earn my "wings".

I was lucky to have Del as my new partner as I took my initial plunge into the world of overhead, bridge operated cranes. Riding around with your loads and sitting above your hook was dramatically different from our belly box job. And Del was a patient, and knowledgeable teacher.

I had a bad dream on the night before I was to start in those overhead crane cabs, high above the floor.

In my dream, I saw my motionless body, laying in a pool of blood on a concrete floor, from an overhead perspective, like from an airplane. Although it was only a nightmare, it shook me deeply. It seemed like a bad sign.

On my first day in the cab, I was already apprehensive, but my baptism in the cranes wasn't complete until I had to crawl out on the roof beams to get out of my cab.

These cranes hadn't been used recently, and lucky me, I got stuck in a broken down cab in the middle of nowhere for four hours.

It felt like twelve hours to my bladder, and I reached the point where the dam was about to burst. The only way out and to the bathroom, was to crawl precariously across the beams that supported the roof.

I made a good "impression" that day. My white knuckled fingers practically dug into the steel, as I hung on for my life. With reruns of my dream, making my heart beat double time, like watching a horror movie.

I got a short preview of working the overheads that day, but the biggest lesson I learned was a crane operator should always make a "pit stop" before entering the cabs.

You don't know when, or if, ever you will see another urinal.

There was a tremendous amount of work to be done moving into this new site, and as crane guys, we were also the "B" forklift drivers on second shift.

This was probably the proudest time of my career at Boeing, as Del and I tackled the workload of a dozen men with just the two of us. I think at that time, I made amends for any "screw off time" I had spent throughout the years,. As we busted tail for weeks on end maintaining production, while bringing the just moved in shop back to order.

We worked straight through most breaks, and took only 15 minute lunches on the run as everyone needed everything done, RIGHT NOW. We were overwhelmed with the work, but we really rose to the challenge. That "Boeing Pride" and can-do spirit had never been more alive, than in the efforts of Del and myself at that time.

But we were hopelessly and woefully understaffed. The shop production was running at full steam and we had more than enough crane work to keep us busy all day. Yet, we had no forklift driver, and we were doing double duty trying to accommodate all of PSD's jitney requirements too.

We had no supervisor on shift, so we were self driven. Our boss, Anna was on first shift. So, we called Plant 2 dispatch, for some forklift help.

That's when I first met Tex, the Plant 2 maintenance and material handling supervisor on second shift. (I'm not using his "real" name. My purpose is not to embarrass or "badmouth" anyone. So, in such cases, the names have been changed, to protect the guilty)

Dressed in a cowboy hat, cowboy boots, and a real "old west" style black vest, he moseyed up, bowlegged, with our General Supervisor in tow.

There was no "Howdy Partner..." in the introduction. Tex was spitting fire.

"Do you mean to tell me you're so 'god damned' busy, that you can't take care of your own forklift jobs...?" he asked, hands on hips, ready to draw his six shooters.

Calmly, but firmly, I replied, "That's exactly what I'm telling you. It's been nonstop for weeks around here. We usually can't even work in a lunch time..."

John, the general, was a reasonable man, and gave Del and I his empathy.

"I know...PSD can be a pretty demanding customer. I'm sure you guys have had your hands full" John said.

Steam puffed out of Tex's ears. He had hoped to demean and crucify us in front of the big boss. But instead he had just demonstrated to our commander, what a blowhard he was. It was a pleasure meeting him. Compared to the displeasure of getting to know him.

He reluctantly gave us forklift support on an "on call", as needed basis. And Del and I were able to focus more on our job title, as crane operators. But it was clear that we needed a dedicated full time forklift driver. Most of the time, the shop's many needs, were on a "take a number" basis.

We didn't enjoy our "popularity", but we were still the most needed employees in the plant. The leads from various departments would fight over who would "get us" first. We did our best to keep everyone happy.

One of the leads, Ben (not his real name either), took his job very seriously. Like the rest, he felt no job was more important than the one that he needed us to do at the time.

But as a crane operator, I felt crane jobs ought to take priority. As we were on our way to help another lead who felt the same urgency about his need, I told Ben, "Call dispatch to get yourself a driver. I'm a crane operator first...."

"Hey, you're whatever I tell you that you are...And right now, I'm telling you that you're my forklift operator"

I appreciated his zeal, but his demands that we be full time surrogate forklift operators undermined our cause of getting the help we needed. We needed forklift drivers, so we could take care of our crane lifts.

Although by contract we were allowed to work out of our job titles for 4 hours a day, we often exceeded that limit. Ben and I would bicker over this daily. And Tex was stingy with loaning out his drivers. One day it all came to a head.

"So...I talked to your boss, and he said you ARE forklift drivers..." Ben declared righteously.

"Oh yeah...What boss was that?" I quizzed, knowing good and well that he hadn't spoken to Anna.

"Tex. He said, that you're to do whatever I tell you to...."

I scoffed. "In the first place, he's NOT my boss. And in the second place, he doesn't know what in the HELL he's talking about...."

I was surprised to look around and see that Tex was standing only yards away, clearly hearing our conversation. Oh well, I didn't care. He wasn't my boss, and Ben wasn't the only lead man around PSD with blazing fires needing to put out either.

"I'll fix those "Prima-Donnas" Tex muttered to Larry, the shop supervisor.

In a sudden charitable move, Tex had volunteered to take on the responsibility of becoming our manager at second shift PSD, the very next day.

He became like a CIA man, keeping us under his constant surveillance.

On one of the rare occasions when we were caught up, I shut off my forklift, and started heading back to the crib for a break, a couple of minutes before break time.

"It's not break-time yet..." Tex growled, lifting his watch.

"Look boss, we've been humping all day, and I'm caught up. There's no lifts to do right now, anyway...."

"I don't care. If you're not craning, I want you driving. Even if you're just hauling an empty tub skid around. What if the superintendent came by...?"

Right Tex...I'm sure the superintendent would rather that I be wasting company gas, than wiping the sweat off my brow, two minutes before our break.

Tex was on a crusade. He redefined the management job. From now on, rather than helping make sure that maintenance and material handling was supportive of the shop's requirements, his main job was to heckle and harass Del and myself. And he was doing an excellent job of it.

Tex wasn't working for the Boeing company anymore. He was working for his own spite. He spent most of his time hovering over us, making life unpleasant, and killing our morale. Except for the times he would return to Plant Two to supervise his own maintenance guys that he was keeping busy... making custom made car parts for his classic Chevy.

If they had an award ceremony for "Dirty Boss of the Year", Tex would have been taken the trophy.

Meanwhile, Ben was loving this "under new management" slavery. With the leverage of Tex backing him up, Del and I were often his personal genies. I took it for a while, but one day I'd had enough.

Ben and I squared off for a wall rattling shouting match, fists clenched, that drew the attention of the whole factory. Larry, the supervisor, patiently waited out the tense ten minute verbal brawl, rather than calling security.

After it was over, we both felt relieved, having cleared our minds and voices of all hostility. Things got better between Ben and I from that point forward.

Also, realizing the futility of Del and I being able to tackle all the forklift and crane tasks, even with Tex blowing fire up our behinds, we got a full time forklift driver, Lee. And as a bonus, they also added an additional crane crew on second shift to help us.

Life was getting better, and production finally had the support they needed and deserved. Finally, every day at work was becoming a "good day".

Well, almost every day. Except for the one day that rolled around every couple of years, when we had to take our company physicals.

14

GETTING THE "FINGER" FROM BOEING

Many jobs, including cranes required a Boeing "Physical" every two years. As the office muzak played Olivia Newton John's "Let's get Physical" in the background, the bald headed doctor did just that.

When you heard the snap of rubber gloves behind your back, you realized that Boeing was about to give you the "finger", to pay you back for going out on strike.

I don't know what this unwelcome intrusion had to do with running our cranes.. I guess they were checking for swollen prostates. I think my prostate ran and hid when he felt the doctor's digit come creepy crawling up there. But the dedicated doctor sure was determined to hunt him down.

They have a blood test called a PSA that would have told of any prostate issues. But that would have been too easy. It was just one of those sacrifices you had to make to wear your crane operator crown. But sacrificing our virginity for the job, did make us feel a little cheap.

It's funny, the doctor seemed to be indifferent as he listened to your heartbeat, or looked in your ears. But then, he really got into the spirit of the exam, when probing our tailpipes.

I don't think they ever found anything, except maybe hemorrhoids which were epidemic from spending so many hours sitting in the crane cabs. Maybe some of the fellas didn't mind this intimacy of this diagnostic test. But I spent all of the two years between exams, dreading the next one.

Paid by the hour, these doctors really didn't seem to care about your "well being", other than really putting in the extra effort on the "well drilling".

Once when I was a safety monitor, I was instructed to tell our crew to call Boeing Medical first, in case of an emergency. I told them that I was supposed to tell them that, but if there was a real emergency, to forget that, and call 9-11 first instead. I didn't trust them. Unless you needed an emergency prostate exam.

I felt that if we called Boeing Medical first, the second call we made would have to be to the funeral home. I pictured the call going like this.

"Boeing Fire department..."

"Yes, you need to get right out here....I think someone's having a heart attack..."

"Okay. We'll be there... right after lunch"

And they would arrive just in time for the last rites.

As safety monitor, I was our designated medic, trained in first aid and CPR. I actually got a chance to use my CPR skills one day at the Thompson site.

I won't mention her name. But one of our janitors, a young lady, had passed out, and her eyes had rolled up inside their orbits. She wasn't breathing. It was just Del and myself in the crib with her at the time.

I felt for her pulse, and I couldn't find it.

"Del, will you check?" I asked. Whether her pulse was just too faint or absent I don't know, but he couldn't detect one either. Some people had started to gather around our crib.

"Does anyone here know CPR?" I asked frantically. No one answered. Although I had been trained, I was hazy on the technique, and not real confident in my abilities. I would have rather someone else take the glory for saving her, or take the blame if they couldn't. But with no takers, it was down to either me trying...or her dying.

"Someone call 9-11", I shouted, and tilted her head back, running my fingers through her mouth to clear any obstructions. Oh man. This was the real deal. I practically had a heart attack, trying to remember how to treat someone with a heart attack.

I pinched her nose, and blew a couple breaths into her lungs. Then I started working on her chest compressions.

"Is it five compressions, then two breaths? Or, five breaths and two compressions?" I tried to recall. My victim was no help at all as she laid there expressionless, fading away into La La land. I just winged it, jumping back and forth between lip locks, and pushing down with my paws between her cleavage.

Suddenly her eyes opened widely, as I was straddling her, with my hands on her chest. She coughed, and her arms lunged up instantly, trying to push me away.

"Get OFF of me!" she cried. I remember from class, them saying if they can talk, they must have a pulse. So she was alive! And most unmistakably, not in the mood for a guy hovering on top of her. This was my worst date ever!

The paramedics from Medic One arrived as did the Boeing Fire department. I let the boys take it from there.

She refused to be transported. I later was told that was because it was some kind of drug induced event, and she didn't want to lose her job. From that point, I became known to our crew, as the "guy who jumped her bones".

While the use of drugs and alcohol were thought to be a sure way to get into trouble at Boeing, it was also a foolproof way to get OUT of trouble at the Lazy B. No matter what you had done, or how deep of a hole you had dug yourself into, saying, "I have a substance problem and need help" was a surefire, "get out of jail free" card.

It was a one time, all is forgiven...."We will help you", remedy to any disciplinary action you might be facing. Boeing would pay for your rehabilitation, and absolve you of any wrongdoing. But only once. If you didn't straighten yourself out. You were through.

I never had a substance problem, and never was I in bad enough trouble to even consider using this tactic. But one day I got a letter in the mail, saying that I couldn't come back to work until I had been cleared by Boeing Medical. Since I had a substance problem. I did NOT!

I hadn't done anything, and I surely didn't want to be probed with the finger by Medical so I could be let back in the gate again. So I called them up. It was another Edward Sweeney who had been rehabbed. And somehow our files had gotten mixed up. Whew! After being acquitted of my drug and alcohol abuse accusations, I fixed myself a well deserved, drink.

Some people were chronic visitors to Medical, getting excused absences for their real or imagined ailments. I'm told that Boeing had a special nurse ready for those people. I never met her, but she would put an end to that nonsense with just a wave of her hand.

"What are you in for today?" she would ask, hands on hips.

"I have a headache"

"Okay, pull down your pants...." She would demand.

I don't know how many symptoms that a pesky prostate can mimic. But I'm told that one exam from this nurse, could cure a headache, for life.

15

PARKING THE JITNEY

The addition of our Jitney Driver, Lee, brought an end to my forklift driving for good. I was now what my job title said I was, a full time crane operator.

Our new colleagues included Moe, who came out of Plant Two, via the pages of a comic book. He was a wacky guy, who amused everyone, but mostly himself, with his imitations of the Road Runner and the Three Stooges. Moe really tried to live up to his name.

Tony, from the Robbins building had also been rehired, and it was great to work with him again. And we also got Tracy, one of Boeing's first female crane operators, on our crew.

Having a decently staffed crew was a relief to everyone. The shop was able to get their lifts done in a timely manner. Del and I weren't frantic trying to figure out how to be five places at once. And with so many witnesses on the crew, even Tex backed off on poking Del and I with his pitchfork a little.

They even added a third shift crew, comprised of Pat and Denny, both of whom I would later work with in the Renton Crane crew. And there was still plenty of work to keep everyone busy.

141

This was Boeing working as Boeing should work. Relaxed, but productive. Well staffed, well oiled, and with reasonably good morale.

In those days Boeing used to sustain that morale with frequent gifts and rewards for a job well done. Accomplishments would be honored with gifts of logo hats, coats, shirts, promoting the company or department, while keeping smiles on our faces.

They also had relaxed the rules on coffee pots and radios, lending to a more amiable, inviting environment to spend a good portion of your waking hours in. Little things meant a lot, and a lot of little things contributed to the big success that Boeing was enjoying.

Ever since the 70s, employee recognition had been waning however. Once upon a time, Boeing would pay up to $10,000 for a good idea that would increase productivity through their "Boeing Suggestion System"

In the midst of 5S, just in time, and productivity committees, Boeing scrapped their suggestion system altogether. Suddenly, a drought of ideas came upon many, as their imaginations strangely went dry.

Yet, on a dark and stormy night, when I worked at the Robbin's site, my boss Mike, felt badly having to send me out to throw fallen tree branches in a dumpster at the height of the monsoon. Mike rewarded me with a big "Maglight" flashlight, that I still cherish to this day.

Tony was flabbergasted, "He gave it to you...just for doing your JOB?" he balked. What? Was I supposed to turn it down? In spite of Tony's sour grapes, that generous gift of a flashlight, sure lit up my face.

All of our crane operators, were much more experienced, and talented than myself. I tried as hard as anyone, but it was a struggle for me to do what came so naturally for them. I guess I had a lot more forklift genes than crane genes in my DNA.

After quite a bit of struggling however, I was finally becoming a fairly decent crane operator. But as expected, as soon as you're happy, things are due for a change. They decided to retrofit our overhead cranes with remote, ground control "belly boxes", which would eliminate half of our crew.

In defense of my job, and on behalf of our crew, I wrote a compelling letter detailing the advantages of the two pairs of eyes with a cab operated crane and a hook-tender giving signals to him. The labor savings could so easily be lost if there was even one mishap on loading these expensive engines.

My management didn't appreciate me circumventing the "chain of command" and addressing my letter to the vice president of the PSD division. And they told me so, unmistakably.

"Get out", Tex told the rest of the crew. Then he and Anna escorted me into the crane crib. Neither were smiling.

Under the lights, Anna asked me sternly, "I just want to know, WHY did you do it...?"

"Because I thought it needed to be said", I answered, unblinkingly.

"Why didn't you just bring the letter to me?" Tex demanded.

"Because I wanted to make sure it got to somebody who mattered. Who could do something about it", I admitted, point blank.

"Well, I would have taken it right to them myself", Tex claimed. Sure he would have...

"I'm not sorry. I believe in everything that I wrote"

Anna finished. "I'm not mad. It was a good letter, and what you said made a lot of sense. But in the future, I'd appreciate it ,if you would go through us instead of sending letters to the head man of another division."

You're the bosses, I thought. If that's the way you want it. So be it. I wasn't trying to make anyone look bad. Just trying to give my "expert testimony", to someone in a position qualified to actually consider those thoughts, and maybe prevent these changes.

The meeting was over. And regardless of the logic I had thrown against retrofitting the cranes for remote control, soon we were running belly boxes with a crew of only two men.

It was goodbye to Moe, Tracy and Tony as the crane crew dwindled back to just Del and I. Soon, Del was able to get a long awaited transfer to day shift at another plant. And I met my new partner, good old Don.

It was an unlikely pairing. Don was a self admitted "redneck". And I was still keeping the 60s and 70s alive, with my long hair, beard, and according to Don, my "hippie" ideas. But despite our differences, we got along great.

The fit check operation had been coming to an end, and our workload had slowed. Del and I used to take turns running out with the belly box to do our jobs. Don had a different idea. We would both go out together on every job.

Don was at least 10 years older than I, and winding down for retirement in the mid to late 90s. So, like Fred from Space Center, he wanted to leave the craning jobs to the youngster.

I did the overwhelming majority of the crane lifts, while Don would hook up my slings, turn shackles, and help me unload my gear. He liked to keep busy. More so than myself.

But Don made up for his lack of craning, in the kitchen. He was a wonderful gourmet chef. Most nights, the odors wafting around the shop from his pan, caused stomachs to rumble with hunger throughout the factory. Ed was well fed.

I had evolved physically since returning to Boeing in 84'. Coming back at pretty much my ideal weight, working as a grunt in the construction crew, had kept me fit. As had lifting all that Xerox paper. Settling into my forklift, had caused the pounds to sneak back in, as I spent more time sitting than on my feet.

I had bought a pair of "Space Suit" looking, insulated coveralls during my first year as a forklift driver. They fit loosely. By the next winter, they were so snug that I was unable to bend in the middle.

Driving around for 5 minutes stiff as an ironing board on the seat of my jitney was a hilarious sight. But it was revealing of the carnage my lower level of activity was wreaking on my physique.

As I expanded my skills in the crane, I was also expanding my butt print on the cab seat. Nevertheless, Don's cooking was so delicious, that I don't regret a single pound that I gained, savoring his blue ribbon dishes.

When in Rome, we did as the Romans. When the work was intense, we had worked intensely. When the work was easy, we took it easy. Rome had come to East Marginal way. Those were some of the most fun times that I ever had at work.

The motors of our cranes had plenty of time to cool down between jobs. As the months passed by, more and more of our lifts were being eliminated. No more fit check. And less crane work was needed on the engine line too. We took our responsibilities seriously, but we had plenty of spare time too.

We watched TV on the "safety film" television. I brought in my guitar and would practice between lifts. We got along well with the Pearlie and the rest of the janitors that shared our crib. We played games. But taking care of the shop was always job number one. Even in Rome.

The great Nisqually earthquake happened during this era, and since there was some damage to be repaired in the factory, operations were suspended at the Thompson site. Everyone was furloughed, with full pay.

Silly me, I made the mistake of showing up, not knowing if this applied to us, under the "maintenance" umbrella. As it turned out, we were expected to show up, but I was one of the few who did. Everyone got paid, even those who enjoyed their "free" vacation at home.

But in the Boeing tradition of recognizing those who go the extra mile, those of us who came in were given an "I survived the Nisqually Earthquake" T-shirt. But no extra gas money for our "extra miles" driving in, while our buddies kept their cars parked at home, getting paid just the same.

Next came the horrible morning of September 11, 2001. We all watched the terrorist attacks on the World Trade Buildings in disbelief. As a nation we were saddened and stunned. The future of aviation looked uncertain. Immediately layoffs were announced.

Congress gave blank checks to the airlines who said thanks, and pocketed the cash while dishing out pink slips. I thought the stipends should have been conditional, making sure the money was used for enacting safety measures that would avoid a repeat of this horrific tragedy.

The skies were eerily free of planes, as we sat next to Boeing field pondering our own fate. The layoffs threatened to cut deeply. Although I had over 20 years of seniority, no one felt immune. Nor did anyone know how many heads would be cut.

With the luxury of our slow workload, I used some of my time to take a couple of online courses. I had always been interested in medicine, I even once dreaming of becoming a doctor. So, I studied medical terminology and Anatomy and Physiology, thinking I might pursue a second career as a Physician's Assistant if I were given the boot.

It never came to that, but it was a time when we waved goodbye to a many excellent employees. I felt lucky to have escaped the chopping block.

We took care of our customers well, and gave them service with a smile. They were happy, and we were happy. But our crane requirements continued to decline. Eventually, all we had left was the 777 engine load.

That meant only a couple of crane lifts a week. I was awfully glad I was paid by the hour, and not by the pick. But the gravy dish was about to lose it's ladle. They were going to cut our two man crew in half.

I had more company time than Don, but in surplussing it doesn't necessarily go by seniority. It was probably because of his cooking. But Don stayed at this "Country Club", while I got my papers to go off to a "real" crane job. In Renton.

16
RENTON...THE REAL DEAL

I've always hated change. In fact, I'm always cashing in my coins for dollars. But changes from a comfortable job, to an uncertain one, are even worse.

I dreaded going to Renton. But on the other hand, by now I had some experience in the overhead cranes under my overly tight belt. It can't be all that bad, I figured. By then, I knew what I was doing in cranes. Or, so I thought.

Even before I became a crane operator, I had noticed that part of the crane "persona", was to be a little bit "cocky". Kind of like the pilots in the "Top Gun" movie, it behooves a guy to walk into a crane job with an air of confidence. "I got this, look out..." is the demeanor that the shops and the other operators expect from a crane operator.

So, when I nestled into the crane in the 4-20 building for my first lift, I grabbed the controls like I owned them. "Here I go..." I muttered to myself. "Just like I used to do at PSD"

Immediately, I discovered these cranes were a whole different animal than the Thompson site's cabs. These beasts were wild, and ferocious.

149

Gone was the smooth, "Give her a little gas, and we'll ease on out there" touch of my Thompson cranes. Just a little tap on the lever, and they were burning rubber. And my hook started swinging, like a playground swingset.

I could have gotten the hang of the takeoffs, and learned how to control the swings. But trying to stop these antique machines, was downright crazy. When you backed off on the controls, they would lock up the brakes, and send both the operator, and his load flying.

Yet, the other operators at Renton LOVED these cranes. Did they not know or understand how a crane is supposed to work and feel? To me, it was like driving in a fuel injected dragster, with a sticky clutch, and no brakes. To stop, you had to slam it into reverse. This was insane.

But to my fellow operators, I was the insane, and unsafe rookie, terrifying the workers below. But they say practice makes perfect. So I practiced and practiced. At the end of my efforts, I had only gotten better at making a perfect buffoon out of myself.

Luckily, I was working once again with Del, and he was well versed on operating these unruly cranes. He did his best to train the un-trainable guy that I was. But rather than developing my skills, I only developed a disdain for the cranes in this building, that would follow me until I retired.

Del is a great guy, but he is a soft spoken man. As he would be trying to explain the techniques and processes to me on the floor, or even in the cab, the ear shattering riveting from the wing line would swallow his words, whole.

"Jskkskk yeesh jfjfjieie", it sounded like he said.

"WHAT?" I would ask

"Jskkskk yeesh jfjfjieie" he would repeat. Again, I didn't have a clue as to the words he had said.

"I can't hear you Del"

"Jskkskk yeesh jfjfjieie" he would say again, a little bit louder.

Tired of this repetitive misunderstanding, I'd take a wild guess at what I thought he was trying to tell me.

"Yeah, okay" I'd say, and I would give the operator the "wrongest" possible signal.

"NOOO!" Del would scream, as the operator upstairs would throw his hands up in disgust, and confusion.

So, we'd do it again. Pretty much the same as the last time. For some reason, given only two choices...the right way, and the wrong way....I had an uncanny knack for choosing the wrong one every time. How I wished I were back on my forklift again.

It's bad enough to be the new guy. But at break time, I felt the stares from my crane partners. Some were angry, some were amused. But clearly I was both the "new guy" and the "village idiot". And I couldn't argue with their assessment.

They were all pretty good guys, but they were all professionals, and proud. They knew their stuff and were damn good at what they did. Any trace of my "cockiness" was long gone, after a couple days of making a spectacle of myself on the ground or in the sky.

One time in particular, I was on my first "two cab" move learning to bring a 737 "Big Inch" tool into a wing jig with Eudicio in the other cab.

The big inch is a mammoth tool, bigger than the airplane wing itself. It's name came from the one inch plate steel material it was made from. Suspended from a pair of overhead cranes, it would make the world's largest battering ram, if used for that purpose.

I didn't mean to, but I almost used it for that very thing.

I was in the "lead cab" being followed by Eudacio, as we traveled toward the jig. An extra set of eyes would be handy for crane operators on two cab lifts, but I barely had one good pair. And those eyes were busy looking behind me, trying to make sure that I was in sync with the other cab.

I'm told, I was heading straight toward the jig with my weapon of mass destruction dangling from my hook. I'm not sure. But the blood curdling screams from the shop floor, as terrified mechanics and toolers ran for their lives, hinted that something was wrong.

Eudacio was pulling back on the reins, slamming his cab into reverse, trying to put the brakes on our big inch. "Whoa baby", I think I heard him shouting, and laughing. This was the most excitement this factory had seen in a long time.

Maybe, I was just trying to make sure everyone was on their toes...ready to correct my course at the last minute. Probably not. But as the new guy I was really making myself famous... And, from then on, everybody DID make sure they were on their toes, when they saw that I was in the cab.

Confidence in me, was understandably at an all time low. Confidence in myself, couldn't have been much lower either.

But Lyle "E" (I have to use his initial because we later had multiple Lyles on our crew, was sympathetic and understanding.

"Don't worry about it Eddy. We all make mistakes. You just have to get back on the horse, and don't let it get you down"

I would have loved to have a horse to get back on. To gallop back to the forklift lot. Where I could hop on a jitney, and know what I was doing.

But Lyle would be my advocate throughout my training, and throughout my entire crane career. He truly reflected that Boeing spirit of "Working Together", that helped the company be the great achiever that it has been.

Many of the guys on the crew, as well as the tooling team that assisted us with the lifts gave me as much encouragement as they could muster. I think they thought of me as their "developmentally disabled" trainee.

Not that I could blame them, after several of my "pioneering" botched attempts to rethink the "right ways" of doing lifts. I appreciated the patience they granted this "special needs" crane operator. "Special Ed" was grateful.

So much so, that after my long grueling training period, when I finally got "certified", (as a crane operator, not a certifiable idiot) I put the whole crew in for recognition points. My boss, Bob, who was finally being able to wipe the nervous sweat I had caused off his brow, gladly approved my request for rewarding my teachers.

But in the 4-20, I was still a fish out of water. I wanted to be a good operator, but I never had the intuitive "knack", that my crane partners all shared. Even with my best efforts, the best I could do with these funny cranes on these odd lifts was barely adequate.

On a good day, I might give myself a "C-Minus". My average was more like a "D-Plus" with an occasional "F" on my report card. I needed to get out of there.

I'm not particularly stupid, but I sure felt like I was. A few guys were willing to hang out and buddy up with their "retarded" friend. Like Lyle E., who had been a rookie here himself one year before me. Steve H., and Chuck O., were sympathetic to me too, and gave me lots of helpful tips. But I never really felt like "one of the guys", in the 4-20 building.

I was never one to get to work much before my time. Nor was I in a hurry to go home. After a shift, I was drained from anxiety, and frazzled from driving in the complicated "fast lane" of the crane runways.

I'd often chat with Scotch, a third shift operator before taking my chances on the freeway driving home. (Scotch is not his real name. I changed it to the name of a famous drink)

"I'm really trying. I want to be a good operator, but it's so different from where I came from..." I cried on Scotch's shoulder (figuratively speaking, there were no real tears)

"I know that you're trying. You know what? You ought to see about coming on Third shift. We have a great bunch of guys, who would take the time to help you get better" Scotch suggested.

"Man, that sounds good. I really need a change. This is driving me crazy. I'm a nervous wreck at the end of each night!"

It was the best thing that had happened in months. There was an operator, Dave "H", on third, who had been seeking on spot on second shift. So we negotiated a mutually satisfying, shift swap.

Best of all, my first training would be starting in a new building. The 4-82 final assembly building. Not in that dastardly 4-20.

Coming on third shift, I immediately felt more at ease. The more relaxed pace was like a dose of Paxil, calming my fried nerves. The guys, Lyle "B", Pat, and Denny, were easy going, and happy go lucky operators.

The cabs in final assembly were sky high, a good 80 feet in the air. But the feel of the controls were just like the cranes in the Thompson Site. Familiar, the way cranes are supposed to be.

Life was good...Until I started on my first "real" lift.

"Come ON! Get that block down here! HIGHBALL!" the ex Marine screamed at me, like I was a boot on my first day in drill camp.

He pointed an angry finger at a precise spot he wanted my sling to land on the floor. Not an inch to the left, not a quarter inch to the right. Right there. My palms sweated, and my fingers trembled, as an endless string of his cuss words echoed in the rafters.

I couldn't blame the guy, really. While I was a thousand times better at operating these cranes than I was in the 4-20, I still wasn't very good. Naturally, as a bona fide crane operator, I was expected to be.

And he was one of the fastest, most talented operators of all. He had the eyes of an eagle. He could not only set his load down on a dime...He could put it right in Roosevelt's nose.

"Which nostril would you like me to put it in..?", he could ask. He could even clean Franklin D Roosevelt's boogers out, without even a hint of a swing in his block.

Once off the job, all was good. Laughing and sharing potato chips in the crib. But when it was crane time...my name was "#$*!!!!&!&" Or maybe '****head".

I answered to either.

Thankfully, one of our jobs was to service the 4-86 building, where we would move 737 wings around with a "belly box". I wasn't fantastic on these moves, but I was more in my zone in remote controls.

There was a schedule to determine who would be the "86" man for the night, but I would often volunteer for it.

"You're in the 86? You want me to take care of that for you?" I would offer eagerly.

"Sure Eddy, thanks!"

It was clearly a win/win situation. Most of the guys didn't care for the belly box work. And I wasn't crazy about getting yelled at in the overheads. So, everybody was happy.

But I did need to certify in the 4-82, so I had to soil the seats of the cabs, trying to get a rudimentary understanding of those big fuselage and wing moves, where the big hunks of metal became airplanes.

It wasn't easy, but I eventually got signed off and approved in final assembly too. The bad news is that meant I would be going back to my troubled home, in the 4-20 building. But there was more good news to come.

Dennis "F" (not Denny), who had moved over to the 4-20 building to make room for my training, LIKED it there, and asked if he could stay. Being the fool in the cabs of the 4-82 was purgatory. But the 4-20 was deep in the heart of hell. I got to stay in Final Assembly in the 4-82.

I did as many trades as I could to stay away from the cabs, and remain in the peaceful, happy belly boxing of the 86 building.

I even nicknamed it, "The Sweeney Building"

But I did have to do some time in the final assembly sometimes. Ducking my head, and dodging the streaking verbal bullets shot up at me from the floor when I didn't do something "just so"

Our boss, Frank "T", was a great guy. He would often bring in a box of Ezells fried chicken to share with us, just "because". Or treat us to a box of "Chucks" donuts to keep his crew's morale up. He was always cheerful and friendly.

Once, I told him that I had been a few minutes late getting in to work.

Frank said, "Ah, we don't worry about that around here. Just don't punch in when that happens"

What a great boss, not only for us...but for the company too. He understood that a little human compassion, grace, and understanding for the small stuff, went a long way toward motivating your crew for the big stuff. His guys would do anything for him. Or for the company, if he asked them to.

But when someone told him that I was getting some flack from the guys when I was working in the cabs, he tracked me down, and he was angry.

"I heard the guys are giving you a hard time...Is that true?" Frank asked.

"Not really Frank. I think the guys are a little disappointed in me sometimes. I'm trying my best, but I'm still struggling sometimes. I understand their frustration. They're all very good at what they do, and I'm kind of the weak link right now. I'm really trying to do better.

"Well, okay. But if they do hassle you, I want you to tell me. I won't tolerate any disrespect on my crew", Frank said sternly

It was noble and kind of Frank, but it was a "fat chance" that I would rat out my union brothers on anything. Throughout my entire career, I never once sought management or HR to solve my problems.

That's just not what we do to each other. There is a blue collar code of trust, that helped us work together. For solidarity among ourselves, and indirectly for the benefit of the company as we team to solve problems, both personal and professional.

My knuckles were always as white as my blood drained face as they trembled on the controls during a "line move" I prayed that I would have an epiphany, and get better. Gradually I did, and eventually became average, or just slightly below average, at operating the final assembly cabs.

But even once I "had it down" sort of, in the cabs...Final assembly was more like a hobby to me. My forte, and my specialty was flying the wings in the 86 building.

I worked with a variety of toolers in the 86. No matter who I was paired with, it always seemed pretty easy going over there.

I wish I could remember his name, but the first guy I worked with was one of the most dedicated guys I ever met at Boeing. He was retired from the Army, and while he was always serious, he was always pleasant too. He helped me work out a few bugs on how I was performing my job, not in a condescending way. But just with the purpose of making me better at what I did.

Next came Jim "M". He looked vaguely familiar, but I couldn't put my finger on where I'd seen him. But he was a fun, lighthearted guy, and we had lots of laughs as we moved lots of wings. He was the "ice cream man" who would reward my good lifts on a good hot day with a good humor bar, from the ice cream machine.

One day, it dawned on me where I knew Jim from. He graduated the year before me from Foster High School. The world is a small place, after all. Also helping us was John "R", an equally friendly fellow who had a souped up antique car that he took to car shows.

Later I worked with Bucky, who had escaped the 4-20 building to come over to the good life in the 86, along with Ron P., from the 82.

One day Bucky announced that Ron would be leaving, and was going to be replaced by someone new. I was disappointed, but Bucky was anxious to fill me in on the particulars of the new tooler who would replace Ron.

"I have to warn you, her name is Sharron", Bucky grinned. (Not her real name, it's close, but changed slightly for anonymity)

"Yeah? Okay. So we'll be working with a girl. So what?" I acknowledged, puzzled by his weird smile.

"Sharron used to be named 'Al'... She used to be a HE..."

"What?" I gulped. "Really...?"

Bucky explained that he used to work with her, when he was a he. He warned me, needlessly, that we needed to be careful about teasing her, or else HR would have our asses.

"Yeah, of course Bucky. I know that...."

I don't care what people do with their hair, or their spare time, in their bedrooms, or with their genders. I don't completely understand, but I try my best to accept, even though I will probably never "get it". I'm just doing a job, and if you treat me right, I will treat you right.

Yet, I was concerned that I might inadvertently, say the wrong thing, or give a funny look at Sharron. I didn't know what to expect.

I talk to, and treat men differently than I treat women. We typically have different sensibilities, and different sensitivities. My joking is liable to be a little more censored and refined when I'm around the fairer sex.

I guess it doesn't seem to be "fair", but it's just the way I roll. This Sharron, I considered as being somewhere between the two extremes. How could I be myself, and how should I behave?

When I got to know Sharron, it wasn't as difficult as I had imagined. While she may have been officially a woman now, she wasn't the least bit attractive to me. Nor was she overly sensitive, when the "shop talk" got a little salty.

I mainly just put the mysterious secret that perplexed me, out of my mind, and treated her like a PERSON I was working with, without regard to gender. It all worked out. We just didn't talk about some things, at all.

The tooling shop kept shuffling around the crews for the 86 building, every so often. Who could follow Bucky, and especially Sharron?

Bucky was replaced by Mark "C" who looked like one of the guys from ZZ Top. And the closest fit they would find for Sharron, was the humorous and flamboyant Chris "T".

This pair was not only highly entertaining, but a couple of the best wing movers in Boeing. Possibly in the world.

Chris was a frustrated comedian, singer and entertainer. He knew hundreds, maybe even thousands of jokes, and he had the comedic timing of Bob Hope.

"What do you call a deer with no eyes?" Chris would ask out of the blue.

I'd never considered that. After thinking it over, I'd admit, "I don't know"

Chris didn't either, as he answered his own question.

"No eye deer...."

And the gags kept on coming. Some of his jokes actually DID make you want to gag. But most of them were as hilarious, as they were plentiful.

Mark, on the other hand was a real card too, but his humor was dark and sarcastic, even sardonic. Like Laurel and Hardy, Mutt and Jeff, Jeckel and Hyde, Mark and Chis were as different as night and day. But they worked well, and laughed well together.

Sometimes, I felt guilty taking a paycheck. Not that we didn't earn out keep. We worked hard, and took good care of the shop. But for these nightly variety shows, I almost felt like I ought to be buying tickets and paying them, rather than getting paid. It was like watching Cheech and Chong, every night.

Once, Mark spontaneously went into an impression of Seattle's local TV gardening host, Ciscoe Morris. I've never seen a better parody impersonation of anyone, even on Saturday Night Live.

"Oooh La La...." Mark shrieked Ciscoe's famous, patented expression, while dancing around with the same jerky, nervous energy that was rooted in the gardening guy's routine. I laughed, until I nearly peed myself. I asked him repeatedly over the years to do an encore. But his Ciscoe act, was strictly a "one night only" performance.

Chris's shtick was nauseatingly bright, cheerful and positive. Mark's retorts were playfully mean, rude and biting, and delivered with a gloomy mutter. They could have filled a showroom in Las Vegas, I thought.

I always dreamed that when we retired, we might start a radio show. I used to throw out an impromptu joke now and then too, but I couldn't compete with these two "funny boys".

So, IF we ever had a comedy radio talk show, I would have to be the straight man. Although, I think Mark is straight too. PROBABLY, even Chris was straight. (I'm joking...Sort of. Chris used to work some "ambiguous gender" bits, into his comedy material also)

Truly, this was the Boeing spirit at it's best. Working together and enjoying it. It's amazing how much work you can get done while your having a good time. No matter what they threw at us, we would come through.

Whenever the shop needed a special, "Honey Do" job, they would first approach Chris.

"Sure we can do that! No problem!", would be Chris's stock, good natured, people pleasing reply.

But when they had to ask Mark, they would be hesitant. Of course we would end up doing it, but not without a bunch of bitching about it. They should have known not to take it too hard. That was just Mark's style. He enjoyed being a little obstinate. Let him have a little fun, and then watch your wishes become our command.

I never got asked. As the crane guy, I just did what the toolers told me. When in Rome, well, you know how the saying goes.

But enough about cranes. Lets talk about changes.

17
ONCE UPON A TIME

Well, it's break time. One of the favorite parts of the workday at Boeing. Rather than writing more about the daily grind I was experiencing on the Crane Crew, it's time to grab a cup of coffee and look back on how things once were at the Lazy B. And how much they had changed up to that point in the new millennium.

Coffee was now pouring out of coffee pots all over the factory, rather than in the poker paper cups from the vending machines. Free enterprise was booming within the factory, as the Coffee Lords set up shop. Offering a variety of coffees, flavored creamers, teas and ciders that would rival Starbucks.

The once forbidden radios were blaring out heavy metal tunes inside the caverns of the fuselages of the airplanes too. Boeing had discovered rather than killing morale and torturing ears with the grinding and riveting clammor, letting people put a little music in their day actually picked up the rhythm of the progress.

Ah, they seemed to be finally learning that a happy worker is a productive worker. In some respects.

They had long ago pulled the cigarette machines out from the vending machine lines. Then, they sent the smokers packing out into the rain for their ciggies when the factories went smoke free. If that wasn't bad enough, they finally eliminated smoking on all company property entirely.

"Give us a BREAK" the smokers cried.

They did, 10 minutes to get out the gate, take a couple puffs and be back at your work station. As the radios blasted, "I can't get no satisfaction"

Coffee is nice, but it doesn't do much to alleviate a nicotine fit.

The old "Suggestion System" where you could earn up to $10,000 for a good idea was now ancient history. They replaced it with a NEW suggestion system.

"I SUGGEST, that you find ways to become more productive, if you want to keep your job" was the new reward system.

One thing about Boeing, once you became an official "Bee", your workplace was your nest. You felt like you OWNED it, as you buzzed around doing your work.

It was your position. This crew was your team. We were territorial, and protective of our turf, and of the members of our tribes. Our footprints wore deep into the concrete floors of our little patch in the factory. And our fingerprints were all over our work. We belonged to something bigger than ourselves. And that something bigger belonged to us as well.

We may have had our own "ways" of doing whatever we did, but this pride of "ownership" meant once we got an assignment, it got done.

There were things you wouldn't want to tell OSHA or your kids about... Maybe our methods were questionable at times. But our results were undeniable. Once we had nestled into our "niches", we soon became experts at doing what we did. Proud, authorities of our chosen fields, who really knew how to do whatever we did.

Did bosses sometimes "look the other way"? Indeed. But, with confidence in our judgment, knowing that we knew what to do. Even if if looked unorthodox or unsanctioned.

The end, most often justified the means. There was some wisdom in "keeping the reins loose", and letting us do what we do well. It wasn't a "free for all", but there was freedom to find unique and comfortable ways to get the job done. Saving the close scrutiny for the things that needed close scrutinization.

I think that it's possible to "over regulate" the workplaces, and work practices. Sometimes, the chefs have their noses too deep in the pot to let the cooks put the recipe together. The proof is in the pudding. As long as it tastes good, who cares how they mix the ingredients?

Once somebody knows how to glue the parts together, seldom does "big brother" looking over your shoulder make a better airplane. Micromanaging just adds frustration and kills morale.

The best, most efficient and productive crews I ever worked on, were the ones where the employees were left to their own device. Proud of what they do, and of their contribution to the finished product. Well versed and trained in their professions. Highly motivated to achieve personally, and as a crew. Well rooted and entrenched in "THIER" jobs. Really owning their departments. And having a little fun along the way.

You just don't see that same pride, dedication and "synergy" in a galley of slaves, cowering, clinging to their tools for dear life. As a whip cracks. Paralyzed by rules, clauses and ever changing amendments.

When you own the job, rather than the job owning you, your best comes out, willingly. Even eagerly. Great things are born out of pride in yourself and the company, not from servitude.

And they made it even more challenging by taking people away from their job duties, to spend hours in committees to talk about ways to get more bang out of their job duties.

Safety was becoming more than a program to keep people from being hurt. It was transitioning to a legalistic system of complicated laws, bylaws and addendums designed to hurt and punish those who were well meaning, but ignorant of the latest regulations.

"Suspend first, ask questions later" was the new motto. One of our most "do right" crane operators, Brent was suspended for a week pending investigation for following the procedures that we had used for years hooking up chains to lift a "Texas Tower"

Admittedly, there was a fall hazard on this particular lift, and it would have been wise to use harnesses. It could have been a great safety moment, where we talked about doing it a safer way, and instigated the plan to prevent injuries.

But instead, an overzealous safety department, backed up by a headhunting HR unit, walked well intention-ed Brent out the gate. Causing him undue anxiety over his fate, and killing his morale. I can't overstate the "injury" to this loyal and dutiful worker, caused by this misguided "safety" action.

Even more ludicrous were some of the safeguards against "theoretical hazards" that put us in even more harm's way.

An example was picking a 737 fuselage out of a work jig. As the airplane rises from it's hole, toolers and hook tenders watched to make sure the airplane body was clearing the jig. As the plane lifted, the 1 inch gap, enlarged to perhaps 8 or 10 inches. before they could step away from the edge of the jig to safety. To the safety geniuses, that represented a "fall risk"

It would take a very skinny person to fall through that tiny crack, and surely no one on the crane or tooling crew would be able to suck it in enough to become small enough to take that plunge. Stringbean didn't work on the section moves.

So instead, they had the toolers station themselves in a step down platform, behind a railing in front of the fuselage. They were in a poor position to observe or assist in the travel of the airplane section from that vantage point.

Furthermore, if there was any kind of malfunction in the crane and the fuselage suddenly lunged forward, they could become trapped there. And the possibility of them being crushed by the mammoth airplane would be many times greater, than the minuscule risk of some imaginary, anorexic tooler wobbling though the tiny crevice in an unlikely, mythical fall.

But ridiculous safety tyranny was replacing common sense at a frantic pace. No one wants anyone to get hurt. But silly safety regulations that look good on paper, often did nothing to prevent injury. While "crippling:" the worker's ability to do their jobs effectively.

The wild, whiskey filled Christmas parties had been gone for decades. The fresh batch of newer employees couldn't imagine such "inappropriate for the workplace" revelry taking place in these hallowed factories. But the old timers reminisced woefully. "It's Christmas. How dare they desecrate our sacred traditions. It's sacrilegious"

But on the way out also were the cookies and donuts that used to bring the smiles to the safety and all hands meetings. And in the cafeteria, if you bought your own cookie, the milk would likely be "fat free". And the gooey impossibly delicious "deep dish apple pie" that used to shed cinnamon fumes from their aluminum trays were being replaced by "healthy choices" in the cafeterias.

"No smoking, no drinking, no junk food? What kind of workplace is this becoming? Is this a CULT?" we would question.

And good old "personnel", with their friendly smiles and helpful assistance in placing you in a job where you would be happy was replaced by the stern, heartless demigods of "Human Relations" Heavy on the discipline, and displeasure of the workers it "served", HR was light on human compassion and mercy.

Gone were the leisurely walks to the tool rooms and stores, as parts and supplies were now delivered, like the pizzas they discouraged you from eating.

"Here's some tools, and celery sticks...You don't need that nasty pizza. Feel free to have some coffee and music. They'll help you work faster. But no smoking, booze, or cussing"

Work was becoming much less fun.

"Oh well, at least we have our pensions to look forward to. And after we put in 25 or 30 years...We can finally get an "inside parking pass. I guess they really DO still love us....", we'd think.

Umm, I just can't break it to you right now what the future will hold. You can't HANDLE it.

Besides, break is over. It's time to go back to the 4-82 and get back to work.

18
FOLLOW THE BOUNCING BALLS

To some down at work, I was known as the "guy who plays with his balls". I had learned to juggle years ago, when my wife was hospitalized with a very serious heart condition. It helped me get my mind off the helplessness that I felt when she was in ICU, being distracted by juggling. And when she got well, I discovered juggling balls was a good way to kill anxiety, and pass the time. Even between jobs at work.

Since I had no one to juggle with, I used to practice "passing balls" by bouncing them off walls, and even fuselages (my balls were soft and fuzzy) as I was standing next to a plane, waiting for the big moment when we would crane the bird skyward. The shop used soft tennis balls sliced down the middle, to cover up sharp edges inside the airplanes.

They kept dozens of them in a bin, and I considered the bin to be my "toybox" So, I had a lot of balls.

As a crane operator, I was fairly good in the 86 on the belly box by this time. Not quite as good in the 82 final assembly on the overheads, but passable. I avoided the 4-20 building at all costs. I just wasn't a good fit there.

The 4-20 was where all the overtime money was at. So, I made less wages than my associates. I wouldn't go to the 4-20 just for the money...Only when I was sent there, and forced to backfill for someone's absence. Or, at those times when the 4-20 was overwhelmed with work.

It had nothing to do with "laziness". It was just a matter of competence. You would think that management would want to place people where they can do the most good, wouldn't you? Specialization, is the cornerstone of any successful team.

Does the Seattle Seahawks coach Pete Carroll think it's a good idea to put Quarterback Russell Wilson in as a defensive lineman sometimes? I've never seen that happen. No, instead he says, "Just keep throwing those touchdowns Russell! I'm going to let those big, ugly guys take care of all the pushing and shoving"

Or when you're going in for surgery, how would you feel if they told you that instead of your heart surgeon, they were sending in some Gynecologist to do your quadruple bypass?

"WHY?" you would ask, while dialing your Priest to come on down to deliver you your last rites.

"Because we want our doctors to be 'cross trained'" they would explain. "We want to keep our physicians nimble, and versatile"

When you're dealing with specialists and specialties, Cross training only serves to make people "cross". I always got a little cranky when they took me out of my "zone". So I was understandably upset when as I was juggling my balls one day, my boss came up and tossed me a "curve ball"

"Eddy, I'm going to send you over to the 4-20 for a month so you can bone up on your skills"

"Aw come on boss....I don't have any skills over there to bone up on"

Those 4-20 guys were the "Top Guns" when it came to doing 4-20 crane moves. Just let me stay here, where I do a fairly decent job, and let me juggle my balls. He wouldn't hear of it.

I was so distraught, that I dropped one of my balls while doing a simple 3 ball cascade. It hit my boss in his foot and he booted it away. Just like this senseless transfer into that miserable building was, it was a real kick in the balls.

But over the next few years, I would be bounced around from building to building, almost as often as my tennis balls were bouncing off the floor.

I honestly tried, but I was never able to progress very much over there in my least favorite building.

In retrospect, I think I might have brought some of my troubles on myself.

As poor as I was on those cranes in the 4-20, I would have been even worse without the constant tutoring and counseling from the tooling crew in that building. While we still had a recognition system in place, I wanted to reward those guys for their endless patience and understanding while they futility tried to indoctrinate me into the practices of that unbearable building.

So, I wrote up the tooling team for those virtues, and put them in for brownie points, redeemable for prizes and gifts.

"What, are you trying to be Robin Hood?", Scotch, my boss emailed me. I caught his clever drift. But was I really, "Taking from the rich and giving to the poor"?

Not at all. Those "merry men", had joyfully tried to teach me and encourage me, even though everyone knew that I sucked over there. Lesser men would have given up on me long ago. They had really put in the extra effort.

"No sir", I wrote back. "I honestly feel these guys deserve some recognition. They've been an invaluable help to me, and I think that team spirit and morale building attitude deserves to be rewarded"

He vehemently disagreed. We had a rather long, gentlemanly debate on this, through emails. And we even chatted about it in person a couple times. I still don't know why he was so resistant to the idea.

Maybe it really did have to "come out of his pocket" But despite my most vigorous petitioning, it looked like they weren't going to get any trinkets from the Boeing Company. So, I thought I'd do a symbolic gesture instead, to show my gratitude.

"Boss, I can see you have no intention of giving those toolers their recognition points. I think they deserve it. I would like to give them a little reward out of my own pocket to show my appreciation, along with a 'certificate', detailing why I'm having to do it this way" I handed him the note. It said something like this:

"Good Guy Points"

It has been a challenge for me to come up to speed on the crane lifts in the 4-20 building.

But it would have been even more difficult without the generous sharing of your knowledge and the patience you've shown me as I try my best to learn.

I would love to acknowledge this team spirit with some points from the company recognition system, yet my management doesn't consider it worthy of an award. But I surely do.

Please accept this small token of thanks for helping me become a better hook-tender and operator. It's the teamwork of teammates like you, that make this company succeed, and make it a great place to work. The least I can do is to buy you a lunch"

Gratefully,
Fast Eddy

Along with the "certificate", I included a $5.00 gift certificate for McDonald's to each of them. I showed the proposed package that I was going to hand deliver to each of those toolers, to Scotch.

Although it didn't mention him by name, the reference to "my management" could have 'hypothetically' made him "look bad" in their eyes. I didn't want any "backlash" over my awards, so I actually gave him the "veto power" before I passed out the presents.

"Is this going to be a problem?" I asked. "I really think they deserve the recognition, but if it's going to bother you, I won't do this..."

"No, go ahead. Do whatever you want" He even smiled. I thought we were good.

But strangely, that's when all my troubles began.

Every so often, just when life started getting good, I would get another set of "walking papers", and I'd be sent back to the battlefield of the 4-20 building again.

When would they EVER learn...that I would NEVER learn to crane over there like the "big boys"? I was beginning to think that my "lesson" was not so much about making me better at running the 4-20 cranes. We all knew that was a lost cause.

What Scotch was really trying to teach me was probably instead, "Don't embarrass your 'SUPERIORS'".

But back then, I sometimes served as a crusader for what I considered to be noble causes. In that time of eroding employee recognition and perks, I thought it was petty to discount my valid call for recognition for these fine men.

MAYBE I was trying to teach him, "Don't embarrass yourself, with your miserly watch on the 'Atta Boy' cookie jar.

But at Boeing, if you have principles, and you exercise them, those principles might be confused with you being a "troublemaker". They say, "You make your bed, you sleep in it".

And Scotch knew that there was no less comfortable bed to me, than in that flea bag 4-20 hotel.

My penance included more than my reassignment to the dreaded 4-20, the "Antarctica" of the Renton plant. My previously overlooked idiosyncrasies, were suddenly in the spotlight too. My interpretation of the attendance rules also came into question.

For years, Boeing had been emphasizing "Just in time" Mostly in regards to inventory not being warehoused, but supplies arriving just in time to be used in the job.

Never one to arrive much before my shift began, I considered myself to be "on time", if I crossed the "finish line" of the guard gate as the start bell was ringing. Just in time.

I was a master at manipulating the speed limits so that I arrived regularly at that precise second, nightly. I may not have had much crane talent, but I was an expert at "time management".

Not that I missed anything. There was usually a brief time at the beginning of the shift, when tooling was accessing the workload, and developing a plan of crane moves before dispatching the jobs. While the operators waited for their dispatch calls to the jobs.

Apparently, of all the things in Boeing that needed to be managed and supervised, my attendance was job number one for my boss.

At the time, we didn't have a clock to punch, and I was on premises at starting time, so I when I submitted my time, it reflected my "punctuality".

I longed for my old boss Mike, who had once argued on our behalf at about my television with the Robbin's building shop supervisor, "Is the job getting done?"

Like I said, I was getting my work done. But when Scotch said, "If you'd like, we can go look up the cameras. And see what time you get into your work station..." I knew he took this thing seriously.

"I work all over the plant. My work station is EVERYWHERE..." I said.

But Scotch didn't embrace my definition of "workplace". In a tie like this, the scale always tips toward the boss.

So, he won this round of "arm wrestling", and I changed my time reports to meet his specifications. Anything to keep the boss happy. But, he still wouldn't be happy until I was sad, and back in those crazy cabs in the 4-20

When I was in the my building, not only was the job getting done, but it was getting done both in my building, and much BETTER in the 4-20 where others who both liked, and excelled at operating, ran those silly cabs instead of me.

But there I was, back testing the patience of toolers and operators alike, in the 4-20. It's was a good thing it was only for a month.

My boss was excellent at keeping track of the minutes and seconds of my start time. He wasn't as good at charting days, weeks, and months of my 4-20 rotation. The month that I was supposed to spend there, turned into the longest one of my life.

It stretched far beyond 30 days, and it wasn't even leap year. I sure hope those guys enjoyed their McDonald's hamburgers from my gift certificate. Because I would have to work years, and pay dearly for patting those guys on the back.

Meanwhile, I had been crossing the days off my calendar, numbering the days, even checking my watch. Counting down, until the day I could go back to the 86 and 82 buildings.

On the 30th day, I was right on time. "Well boss, it's been a month..."

"Yeah, well let me see how I can shuffle people around to get you back over there. Give me a couple days"

After two more grueling days, I was back knelling before my supervisor again, begging. "Did you decide what you're going to do? May I go back home now?"

"I'm still working on it"

Soon, it was way beyond two months in the 4-20, and again I confronted him. "How about it, boss?"

"Hmm, let me ask (the guy who replaced me) and see if he's ready to come back..."

Oh, so HE gets to decide what he wants to do? How about me? I guess I had nothing to say about my assignment. Those $5.00 gift certificates from McDonalds, were becoming the most expensive hamburgers that I'd ever bought.

But I waited about a week, to see what this trainee who had taken my spot had to say. Maybe he really did need that extra time, to learn the drill over in final assembly.

"He doesn't want to come back. He likes it over there" Scotch informed me. Matter of factly, with no sense of betrayal, or any ethical guilt about going back on his word to me. It wasn't about "training " this man anymore, it was about him having his choice of preferred work sites.

My mouth dropped open. "He can't be serious" I thought. He continued to stare blankly at me. He was serious. I'm sure my supervisor was just thinking, "Are you getting it yet? If you want things to go the way you want, then don't CROSS your BOSS"

"What a GYP", I thought. What do I do now? I could have launched into a tirade, raving about the unfairness of it, and about my unhappiness at being deceived.

But I quickly ran through the "raising hell about it" scenario in my mind. And the preview showed me it would not only be futile, but it would probably only make matters worse for me. Clearly, I would have to become creative, to find my way "back home" to the 4-82

I talked to the guys to see if anyone over in the 82, final assembly wanted my dream gig over in the hellhole of the 4-20. I was delighted that one of our fairly new operators, Tyler, was becoming homesick for his old spot in the 4-20. So, I had to negotiate my own deal.

When I came back, I was back living in my "fairy tale" work life once again. Except this time, it was the story of Goldilocks and the Three crane operators.

"Who's been sitting in my chair...?"

It was the trainee. He wasn't a bad guy, but obviously he was my replacement. While I was singing, "Hey it's good to be back home again", my old crew was singing, "There's a new kid in town". I'd been "replaced", and things would never be the same again.

I was happy to see everybody, but no one seemed particularly glad to see me. Everything had changed in my absence. The only good thing, was that my boss had now been sent on a "special assignment". What his responsibilities were, I had no need to know.

Maybe he was to be the secret agent in charge of watching the gates for the "just in timers". Good pick if that's what it was. But at least I was back in the 82, to stay.

Maybe as an "outsider" since my chair, and my friends had been hijacked. But I'd rather be an outsider INSIDE my favorite building, than an insider in that brutal 4-20 prison.

AND, to my pleasant surprise, the temporary boss who was filling in for Scotch was a friend, Bobby. Bob had been my most patient trainer and advocate during my seemingly 40 years of wandering in the 4-20, And I couldn't think of a better boss to report to, here in my "promised land"

Meanwhile, my buddies over in the 86 building, Mark and Chris, had also been reassigned. Some of their colleagues thought that they were "having too much fun" there. So, there was a rotation of new toolers in the 86 building too. Who neither shared our love for working together, nor had the same affection for this building, and our tasks within it.

It seemed like just another demoralizing change to disrupt job satisfaction, and make sure there was no excess of enjoyment in the factory. After all, work was supposed to be work. Keep your smiles for your own time.

But I made the best of my lot in life. I would still favor the 86, and seize every opportunity to relieve anyone who would rather be working the big cranes in final assembly. Surely, good old Bobby wouldn't mind.

I'm pretty sure that he didn't...But he was possessed by the soul of the manager that he was filling in for. Soon, he too was enforcing our schedule and making sure I wasn't bringing happiness to my crane partners, by swapping duties for their shifts in the "Sweeney Building", the 86.

But overall, Bobby was an upbeat, positive leader. Well liked by both his own crew, and the shops that we supported. He'd been a great operator, and was doing an equally fine job as a boss. Other than minimizing my time in my namesake building, that is.

And like I said, I don't believe that was his own doing. He was only the surrogate, acting in accordance with the wishes of our real boss...who remained "pissed" about my McDonald's certificates, years later. Those burgers hadn't turned out to be a very "Happy Meal" for me. I would continue to eat crow forever over those Big Macs.

Speaking of meals, one of my lunches brought me another few years of teasing and ridicule.

Usually, I would hang my sack lunch on my front door knob, so after showering I would be sure to grab it on my way to work. Something went haywire one day, and instead of my salad, soda, and sandwich, I opened up my lunch bag to discover a couple cans of Alpo Dog food instead.

Boeing's hardest worker, Lyle "B", was quick to seize the sight of my canine diet, and razz me about it.

"Whatcha got for lunch there, Eddy?"

"Ah, I guess it's going to be meat by products today, Lyle... Benji's at home enjoying my sandwich..."

From then on, instead of "Hello", Lyle would greet me with a "Woof, woof" and a laugh. I think it was a needed diversion for Lyle. As he was ruthlessly browbeat by Mike, and others all the time. I was happy to take a little harmless ribbing, to let him not feel so alone in his harassment.

"L.B.", a reference to him carrying a few extra pounds was one of Mike's titles for Lyle. But it was mild compared to the Indian name that Mike had given him, "Big Shadow"

Lyle B, indeed was the hardest working guy at Boeing. He was officially a day-shifter. But his presence was felt almost as often on the second and third shifts too, as he would break Boeing's records for the most overtime worked.

179

He was a frequent fill in for me too, as I was often sidelined with my frequent, debilitating sinus headaches. The guys on my shift probably saw Lyle more often, doing my job, than they saw me.

Subsequently, I was one of the poorest guys working at Boeing, after being off so often on unpaid, "Family Leave". And Lyle, was in turn, one of the wealthiest hourly guys, his paycheck bursting with all those double and time and a half hours. But he sure earned it.

So, we had our two Lyles, Lyle "E" and Lyle "B". Both of them were great guys.

And there was Tim, one of our most vocal crane operators. He had pretty strong opinions on most everything, and he was always glad to share them. I got along well with him, too. Like many, he had talents outside of his crane skills too. Tim had built a house from scratch, in Chelan.

We eventually drafted, Chuckie from the 4-20. He was the guy I mentioned earlier who had once worked in the mail room. Chuckie was a former baseball pitcher, who had once played for a Chicago Cubs, farm team.

It seemed like all the guys had interesting skills and or hobbies. Clay from day shift, had built his own log cabin. Cal had once been a full patch member of a motorcycle club. And I think that I was the only guy at Boeing who didn't have either a Harley or a snowmobile, or both.

I would stick around at the end of the shift to shoot the breeze with some of my day-shift colleagues like Dave "H", and later with Roy "R", after Dave retired.

These guys didn't know how challenged I was as a crane operator. So we could converse and laugh as "equals". I never worked overtime, so they had no idea that they were working with a "developmentally disabled" operator. I wanted to keep it that way.

Brent, the guy who had kept my seat warm while I was in the 4-20 building, and then kept it for himself upon my return, was a long time veteran of the tooling crew.

But he was new to the cranes. He had been the Lyle "B" of the tooling crew. The hardest working, most helpful guy they ever had. And he had really excelled as a crane operator too. In less than a year, he had by far surpassed the abilities I had obtained over my last 20 years.

In fact, I felt I got along pretty good with all the guys. But they were all much more talented operators than I would ever hope to be. Everything would be fine though...if they would just keep me in final assembly. Or in the 86 building. ANYWHERE but in the 4-20.

But the bouncing balls were about to roll over there again.

"Eddy. I'm going to send you over to the 4-20 building again..." Bobby announced one day, out of the blue.

"No you're not", I challenged. Not Bobby too...I lamented.

"Yes, you need more cross training" The voice was Bobby's, but the words were obviously coming from someone else.

As Bobby was a temporary boss, I figured, the puppet strings were being pulled by my "real" supervisor. I guess he must have heard that I was getting "too cozy", where I was.

"No I don't" I challenged. "I'm doing fine over here. Let the 4-20 guys who love their building take care of the 4-20 and let me stay here"

"No, Eddy. I need to make sure you're up to speed in case you work overtime there. I've got to send you over"

"I don't work overtime there. I hate that building."

"I know you do, but I have to send you"

181

FAST EDDY

"No you don't...." I said, defiantly.

"Yes I DO!" Bobby argued, getting a little agitated.

"I'm not going" I insisted. I probably sounded a little like a whiny 5 year old, but I really wasn't about to go back there....

"YES, you ARE" he yelled. I was taken aback. I had never heard Bobby actually holler angrily before.

"No I'm not....." I started to rebuttal. There was an exasperated pause from Bobby.

"I'll just retire" I finished.

It would have been a little premature. But I was only a couple years away from being 60 anyway. I could have retired, taken a little less on my pension for doing so, and been able to tap into my 401K in less than two years. That's how much I disliked the 4-20.

Bobby sensed I was serious about hanging up the towel, and our discussion became calmer. He challenged me to stick around, and promised me my 4-20 excursion would be a short one.

"It's only for a month...Come on Eddy. It'll be over before you know it" I'd heard that one before.

"Listen Bobby, I just don't do well over there. I'm not all that crazy about cranes in the first place. I probably should have stayed on the forklift crew. I'm just kind of burned out on the whole thing. I really think I will retire"

Cranes was a great job, even in the 4-20. High paying, relatively easy work. Even a little prestigious among hourly jobs. Many would say I was crazy for taking the stance I did. "You ought to be grateful for having such a good job..." some would claim.

It's hard to argue. They would have had a valid point. But regardless of money, benefits, and good working conditions, it's hard to put a price on happiness and job contentment. I wasn't ecstatic about being a crane operator anyway. And far less so, in the 4-20. If I were good at what I did, that would be another story entirely. But I just didn't have the "chops" for it, honestly.

After further negotiations, I reluctantly agreed to not turn in my badge just yet, and returned to the purgatory of the 4-20, for my last assignment there.

Finishing up the miserable month, my balls bounced back over to final assembly again, for the last time. Bobby was a man of integrity, and he fulfilled his promise to not leave me misplaced in that hated 4-20 building.

Once back at home in final assembly, I figured I would just tough it out and try to juggle my balls through another few years until full retirement.

But I didn't know that fate was going to bring my history with the Boeing company to a conclusion in the next couple of years.

And it's time for another break, to reflect upon the history of the Lazy B up to that point in time.

19

FROM TREES, TO TRIPLE SEVENS

Everyone who worked at Boeing, even me...was a part of the history of one of the most successful companies in the world. Like grains of sand on the beach, each of our roles was minuscule. But without the efforts each of those tiny grains, the waves would have crashed on some pretty rocky shores.

The flight of the Boeing company began in 1916, three years before my father was born. Like my Dad, Bill Boeing was intrigued and fascinated by aviation.

In Boeing's time, airplane manufacturing was just in it's infancy. It hadn't been long since the Wright Brothers had first taken off in their primitive airplane in Kitty Hawk North Carolina, when Boeing took his first flight.

Boeing had made a boatload of money buying timber land in Grays Harbor, and shipping the lumber to the east coast, via the Panama canal. So he took some of his wealth and started building boats.

He had recently purchased and learned to pilot an airplane. It was a seaplane manufactured by Martin. He and Conrad Westervelt had already discussed building better airplanes, before Boeing's own personal plane had been damaged in a crash.

So they dismantled the wreckage and studied the design, incorporating various improvements such as greater wingspan, improved pontoons, and lighter weight.

They modified their small shipyard into an airplane factory and began using their former ship builders as airplane mechanics. With Westervelts engineering help, Bill Boeing was soon taking their first product, the B and W, on it's maiden test flight himself.

Initially called the Pacific Aero Products Company, the company was soon renamed the Boeing Airplane Company. Boeing was a 75% owner of the bank that financed the company's launch, so getting a loan was pretty easy.

Demand for the exciting new invention of airplanes was already brisk, but the the start of World War One brought promised a bright future for military airplanes. Boeing quickly secured contracts to build planes for the Navy.

The end of the war, canceled the bread and butter contracts for all airplane manufacturers, including Boeing. The market was flooded with used airplanes from the war, and the future of aviation manufacturing went into a tailspin. Resourceful Bill Boeing, returned to building boats to keep the company afloat.

And he even began building bedroom furniture and armchairs to survive the slump. With the future of his company uncertain, he even considered building Ouiji Boards. These were lean times for Boeing, and he began paying employees out of his own pocket, or with company stock. Thankfully, he wasn't about to throw in the towel.

But he also pursued two different markets for his airplane business. Both air mail, and passenger travel utilized the new B-1 "flying boat" design. The 1920s were prosperous years for Boeing as they dominated the fighter plane industry with the PW-9 and the P-12 fighters.

The company was not only building planes, but it merged with Pacific Air Transport and became an airline. It was renamed United Aircraft and Transport. They also acquired Pratt and Whitney, who built propellers and engines.

Boeing might have become the "Amazon" of the skies, doing and selling it all. But anti trust legislation forced the company to break off some of it's business divisions into their own entities. That left United Airlines to fly the friendly skies, Pratt and Whitney to sell engines to Boeing, and Boeing returned to building planes.

Even in the depression years of the 1930s, Boeing was innovating new products. The variable pitch prop design of the Monomail, the modern 247, and the "flying boat", the Clipper, began making transatlantic passenger runs. But the early 1940s were truly Boeing's years of flying high. The later years of the 40s. not so much

It's been said that, "War is hell". But when you manufacture B-17 and B-29 bombers in the biggest World War to date, commerce wise, war is heaven. Facilities were expanded and production went into fever pace.

The building tops were disguised to look like peaceful neighborhoods to confuse enemies who might fly over the Puget Sound region in search of strategic targets. Luckily, our enemies never flew over Seattle.

But in the aftermath of the war, times were hard. 70,000 workers were given "pink slips". And NOT the kind that you wear. No gifts of clothing, but termination papers instead. Sales of the commercial products were sluggish for the rest of the 1940s. But the "happy days" of the 1950s were just around the corner.

The KC-135 Stratotanker and Boeing's first commercial jetliner, the 707 reignited the Boeing fires in the 50s, as well as entering the short range guided missile market. The jet age had also made Boeing a leading producer of gas turbine engines.

In the 1960s, Boeing added helicopters to it's flying fleet with it's acquisition of the Vertol company. The 60s was a progressive time for Boeing as they ventured into space, building the S-IC stage of the Saturn V rocket. They added the 727 to it's airplane line and became the first manufacturer to sell over 1000 units of a jetliner.

Other projects, big and small included the baby Boeing, 737, and the jumbo jet, 747. Both of these were destined to become legendary planes in the Boeing legacy.

As the unlimited hydroplanes roared around Lake Washington in the Seafair cup, Boeing was busy building hydrofoils too, for both civilian travel and military purposes. But the upcoming 1970s would prove to be a challenging, trying time for Boeing.

After finally reaching the moon in 1969, interest and investment in space travel waned. A recession had hit in 69 and 70, and the company had no new airplane orders at all for over a year. The promising 747 had been plagued by engine problems after the company had spend a fortune developing it, and building factories.

And in 1971, Uncle Sam pulled the funding away from the Supersonic Transport (SST) program, ;leading to 60000 layoffs. It looked like it was going to be lights out in Seattle, as a billboard suggested "the last person leaving Seattle" should shut off the lights.

Later in the decade sales, of the 747 began to reflect what a great airliner it was. The "SRAM" and "MINUTEMAN" missile projects also added to Boeing's piggy bank. And Boeing entered the mass transit business, building the "Morgantown", light rail vehicles.

The 1980s, had Boeing back on a trajectory toward super stardom again. Two new airplanes, the 757 and the 767, were highly successful. Boeing was also involved in propulsion for the Space Shuttle project and was a contractor for the International Space Station. The stealth B-2 bomber went into production too, employing 10,000 people in that business unit alone. The good times were back.

It was also a time of excess. I guess you get a bigger bang out of a $600 hammer than a hardware store special, but that's what Boeing was nailing the Air Force for. Meanwhile my union brothers and sisters were carefully scrutinizing the wallet of CEO Frank Shrontz.

I am, and was all for the solidarity of the Union and securing the best deal we can, but much of the propaganda regarding this labor dispute revolved around Shrontz's salary. Looking at the millions he was paid, the implication was that Boeing was being cheap towards the Machinists.

"If they can afford to give Frank millions, then they ought to pay us millions too" was the impression our advertising suggested. Hey, we did a pretty good job, and probably most of us worked more "overtime" than Shrontz.

But let's BE Frank... I doubt they could really afford to pay us ALL that much and still have money left over for our hats, jackets and sleeping bags.

But, if our Union was able to get us seven figure wages, I would commend them. The comparison seemed a little invalid to me, however.

At issue was also overtime. As things got busier around our factories, many nestled into their workstations for what seemed like unlimited periods of forced overtime.

Settlement occurred right before Christmas in '89, and Frank did become sort of a "bribing", Santa Claus, No seven figure salaries for us, but we did get double digit percentages of bonuses to merry our holiday season. And limits on overtime were also enacted.

In the 90's, Boeing was roaring also. Getting a piece of the Advanced Tactical Fighter, continuing to sell lots of our airplanes, introducing the 777, kept the money rolling in. But there was constant rhetoric over competition from both Airbus, and defense contractors, hinting that the traditions of the "Lazy" B, were about to become a thing of the past.

Seeing how the Japanese manufacturers were taking over the automotive industry, Boeing and other companies began peering over their shoulders, to see how they were doing so well. The time honored, "Yankee Ingenuity" was becoming passe, and we were being introduced to "Deeming" principles and the methods used by Asian companies to achieve their dominance.

As all this was happening, Uncle Bill Boeing's offices were about to leave the great Northwest. And soon we were just another outpost of Chicago's Boeing Headquarters. We were now the dysfunctional children of our broken home.

As Boeing expanded it's operations in new locations, they began to look at the Seattle kids as the "naughty ones". Our strikes were viewed as tantrums from spoiled, ungrateful, brats who would throw our plates, crying for our desserts.

I had given my tooling friends McDonalds to reward them for their kindness and help. But our tough new CEO, Harry Stonecipher punished us with McDonnells, as we merged with the McDonnel Douglas company. A troubling new paradigm for company / union relations was emerging.

There would be no more, "Come on Uncle Bill...Give us some candy, and we'll put down our picket signs and get back to work..."

Instead it was, we'll divide and conquer the Union membership. Testy, greedy strikers had become the "bad guys" and the anti union, "You don't know how good you have it" workers were the apple polishing favorites of the new administration here in Seattle.

And our leverage of stopping work to convince the company to see it our way was being countered by the companies own leverage.

Starting in the 90s and continuing on until I handed over my badge, the company was more adamant about "we'll decide what's good for you"

They changed the radios to play, "Just be thankful, for what you've got", as they bumped up their threats.

"You'll take what your given, and LIKE it.... Or we'll take our ball and go somewhere else. Down in North Carolina, they love to play, and they don't challenge our rules...."

They began "farming out" more and more of our work. Some of these experiments turned out disastrously, I'm told. Costing the company far more than they saved by the time the parts were reworked into usable ones. But they were doing more than bargaining for a better deal. They were marketing a new "philosophy" in labor / management relationships.

In some regards, the future mimicked the past, as the factories returned to the old fashioned ways of the early 20th century. Trimming wages, benefits and job satisfaction under the constant duress of "take it, or take nothing".

A corresponding downward shift in pride, loyalty and love for the company accompanied this new deal.

Time will tell, but I think in the long run, workers giving their best because they "want to" has more value than doing what is required because they "have to".

But what do I know? I was just a forklift driver who had gotten lost, and wandered into the cab of a crane.

What I THINK I know, is that these changes were the poison that killed an intangible asset that made Boeing great in the first place. That old "can-do" Boeing Spirit.

I saw that spirit as recently as in the 2000s. When one of our crane bridges failed, it looked as though we wouldn't be able to complete our line move. Even our supervisor looked at the situation and declared, "Well, we're screwed. There's no way we can get this done until the bridge is fixed. You guys might as well come down"

I'm not as smart as these guys, but some of my colleagues wouldn't accept that answer. I remember especially Tim and Mike "P", from the other building putting their heads together and brainstorming about how we could accomplish this job while lacking one of our bridges.

The answer was not clear to me at first, but amid the thunder and lightning of these knowledgeable crane operators reflecting on their years of experience, they ran the gamut of all possible ways to get the plane from point "A" to point "B".

Their imaginative solution saved the day, and saved the company a lot of money. The plane was delivered into the jig, and the production workers were able to proceed, as our mechanics repaired the bridge the next morning.

Again, I cried for recognition for everyone who had collaborated on this heroic "workaround". I wasn't a part of coming up with this means of accomplishing the impossible, but certainly these guys deserved a medal.

I don't even think they got a simple, "Thanks" for their brilliance. I was extremely proud of their dedication and creativity that "saved the day" for the company. But they received no recognition at all. It was considered "Just a part of doing your job"

I WOULD have given them "Big Macs" and a nice letter of thanks, but I didn't want to return to the 4-20 again for being a "wise guy". So, I just personally gave them a well deserved "pat on the back"

Mike and Tim, were the big gravel that day on the shores of the Boeing history. But as appreciation for such dedication dwindles, and Boeing puts bigger locks on the cookie jars, I expect to see such notable rocks on the shores of Boeing erode, and the grains of sand get smaller and smaller.

In the aftermath of my friends saving the day, Boeing stock goes up a point. But a tear forms in Bill Boeing's eye, as the pride and recognition of accomplishment fades.

20
JUST YOUR TYPICAL BOEING GUY

Larry Q. Lunchbucket, your average Boeing blue collar worker was hard to pigeonhole. He's was among the most ambitious workers who ever worked, and he was as lazy as a sloth. He was as brilliant as Einstein, he was not quite as smart as your average rock. He was highly educated and well rounded, he was ignorant and one dimensional. He was fit and trim, and he was well rounded.

It took all kinds, and whether above average or below average, it was hard to find that average Boeing hourly worker. But being in the mill of the Boeing machine for a few years seemed to average us all out. One would either find some conformity to the group, or else become an outcast.

So those with high ideals, would become a bit jaded. Those who lacked ambition, would discover their inner zeal. Those who thought too highly of themselves would find a little humility. And those lacking confidence would learn that they were part of the team too, with something to offer.

Despite our fabric when we came in, we would soon be molded to resemble those who surrounded us. Boeing workers were not born, they were made.

We would come in quite different. But then meet in the middle somewhere beneath the wing of an airplane. And more than individuals, we would be part of a crew with a common goal.

Some came into Boeing as a stepping stone to bigger and better things. Then decided they liked it so well, that they stayed. Others had found the grass was greener on those concrete floors than it was in their chosen fields.

My brother Tom built plastic models as a kid. He worked hard in school, graduated with honors, and went on to the University of Washington. Upon graduation, he shifted gears from his science and psychology education.

Going to Boeing to make some real money before moving on, he discovered he loved his job making models in the model shop to fly in the wind tunnel. And stuck with it until retirement.

My friend and former crane trainer Del, followed in his father's footsteps and became an crane operator just like his dear old Dad. And Del's sons followed him through the gate, carrying on the family tradition.

My bandmates and I had looked at Boeing as a means of acquiring capital to invest in ourselves as the next Rolling Stones. When we learned that Mick and Keith weren't about to step aside, three of the four of us returned to the Lazy B.

My Dad had always told me, "You better knuckle down and get those grades up, or you'll end up digging ditches"

His prophetic words came true, as I found myself in GCU, with a shovel in my hand. I set my sights on better things, and found my niche as a forklift driver. I was happy as a clam, but greed pushed me into the seat of a crane. It changed my Salsibury Steaks into Rib Eyes, but surely softened the smile on my face.

Like many, my early work friend Bob from Hazen High School, was disillusioned after his layoff. And carved out his future by excavating with his own backhoe for the rest of his working days.

Some others found the pace too slow at Boeing and moved on to other careers outside the company. Some succeeded, others didn't.

But those of us who had survived the layoffs and nestled into our grooves, found ourselves as a part of something bigger.

Whether it was collectively maintaining our wages and benefits through our Union, as others watched their middle class lives flounder, or shaking the work dust off our clothes as we watched a 737 taking off, knowing drops or our sweat was dried on those wings, we reveled in the power of what we could do together.

Boeing adopted "Working Together" as their slogan during the 787 Dreamliner launch. And they firmly believe in the virtues of teamwork. But as of late you never hear their earlier idiom, "People are our most Valuable Resource"

Working into the 2000s, we had to face it. If Boeing COULD build airplanes without people, they definitely would rather feed their robots electricity and oil, than pay us wages and benefits, and having to deal with our personalities.

Their "ideal" worker, is a far cry from the ones who put Boeing on the map during their formative, "wonder years". The old piss and vinegar factory guys, who would fight one another to get their jobs done, are no longer welcome inside.

The working together the company seeks is with clones of passive, compliant drones, who work together as a small team. Each of them, in an exclusive partnership with Boeing. Not with their fellow comrades.

Boeing values loyalty. But not the loyalty of one Union brother or sister to each other. Only loyalty to the company who pays them. They'd rather have you "rat out" your colleagues, than cover for them.

And taking them aside for a stern pep talk about getting their act together.

About the time I retired, I saw their latest inspirational posters. Two little kids, one sad little boy with a little girl putting her arm around his shoulder. With a sympathetic look of concern, the caption expressed her comforting words, "I've got your back"

In reality, what many of us felt was that the statement wasn't quite finished. "I've got your back, and I'm going to put a knife in it..." Was more succinct and to the point.

Workers no longer feel as though they are assets, but instead a "necessary evil" to their employer. A continuing trend of making cuts in employee perks went far beyond getting stingy with hats and t-shirts. They closed down the beloved employee gym at the Oxbow. Company sponsored employee clubs are few now.

But the most revealing demonstration of management's waning love for it's employees, was when during the height of record profits, they decided to freeze our pensions and suspend future contributions to the funds.

The media, the aerospace analysts, even many of my friends were unsympathetic. "It's happening all across industry. Pensions are passe"

But Boeing was always better than that. So were it's workers. In hard times, we had sacrificed along with the company. But in good times, when they extort their own neighborhood people who had grown up with the company, it became crystal clear, "People are FAR, from being their most valuable assets"

Old seasoned workers who had given their lives to the company sneered as the company bullied, "Screw you. Take it or leave it. If you don't like it, we'll build our planes elsewhere"

What a brilliant, but sinister plan. Pit young against old. Dangle some inciting cash bonuses in front of hungry young noses, to write off 70 years of collective bargaining progress. In a decade long agreement, that guarantees labor peace, but sells out your future.

That unscheduled contract extension declared the 98 year partnership between Boeing and it's home town workers, officially dead. It was no longer a cooperative association between labor and management, it was fascism at it's best. Leadership by fear and intimidation.

Corporate aristocracy hadn't had it so good in America since the 1800s.

I loved this company, as most of us had. Sure we had our slack times, but we also had our bust tail times. We would all have done anything for the legacy that Bill Boeing had built. A man who would dip into his own pocket to help keep his workers paid in the hard times.

But these new monsters that have taken the reins of his company, would kick our families to the curb, in order to change their dollar bills into fives. As the Company enjoyed it's record profits.

As far as the love affair goes, "The thrill was gone"

Many of us retired, as the company put out ads for "Spineless, docile employees willing to sell their souls to build airplanes. Pay and benefits depending upon our level of greed at the moment. Will train"

It's often been said, "You get what you pay for". And time will tell. But in the long run, I'd bet a few of my pension dollars that these browbeaten, passive. new hire mannequins , won't have half the heart for the company, that our motley crew of malcontents that the company disillusioned once had.

But at least Boeing finally has a staff of "average employees" That all look alike, think alike, and hide the same sense of bitterness beneath their frightened, "Yes sir" robotic facades.

Let's see how that works out for you.

Now retired, I'd rather reflect on the "Heroes" that I'd met throughout my career.

21

A HANGAR FULL OF HEROS

Boeing was like the Justice League of America, full of heroes. From our founder, Bill Boeing, who believed we could make a better airplane, to our engineers who proved that we could, time and time again. To Tex Johnston, who upon taking a 707 on a joyride including a speculator barrel roll over Lake Washington, proved just what our better planes could do.

But to me, some of the ones who wore capes were virtually unknown. My first work hero was my first lead-man, Dick. Why? Because he clearly illustrated to me, as a wet behind the ears youngster, what a true blue collar working man looked like. He taught me how to spray paint, sure. And about all the mechanics of being a painter, too.

More importantly, he taught me how to enjoy working. To work seriously, but to never forget to have a little fun, whenever you can. There is no reason why productivity can't be mixed with laughter and enjoyment. Dick taught me that from day one. Prior to coming to Boeing, I thought that work was a necessary "evil". Thanks to Dick, I discovered that good times, make the "evil" a little less sinister. And that coming to work can be a happy way, to make money.

My next hero was Steve H, who was the first boss to stick up for me in front of a General supervisor who was snorting, and crying for my blood.

True, I was abusing the system a little, when it came to punching in, by chronically clocking in on "grace". But as he said, I was a good worker, and my heart was in the right place.

So, Steve risked his own neck, by refusing to write me up. Steve taught me much about "grace" and loyalty, even in a management to hourly guy relationship. And with guys like him, there was no favor too big, that his dedicated crew wouldn't do for him.

When I worked at the Robbin's Site, I was still kind of a last minute arriver. And on one particular day, the roads surrounding the plant were flooded.

But I was on the verge of getting a "CAM" (corrective action memo) because a few of my "last minute" punch ins, had occurred a couple minutes after the last minute. So I had to risk plowing my Ford Pinto through the small river that was raging where the road used to be.

Some cars were making it through. Others had stalled in the drink. The tide of water was running about two and a half to three feet deep, it appeared.

I would have made it, if everyone had just chugged along, nice and easy. But some moron, with a big monster truck, was doing his best to keep up to the speed limit. He had lots of clearance beneath his rig, but his big bulldozer tires created huge swells.

The wake splashed up to the top of my driver's window, and my engine sputtered out in the middle of the drink. Just as the clock hit 2:30 pm, my starting time.

Not only was I going to get that "letter" I was trying to avoid. But I also had a swamped car I needed to somehow get to the parking lot before I could even go into work.

Thanks a lot buddy.....

As I opened my door to get out and push my dead car, water streamed inside drenching the carpets, seats and upholstery. And I too, was soaked up beyond my waist.

I'm not a small man, and I've pushed bigger cars than my Pinto all by myself. But when your car is full of water, it's considerably heavier than it is when dry. (Trust me on this, don't try this at home)

And when you are tying to push that overweight waterlogged car THROUGH WATER....a little Pinto weighs more than a thoroughbred racing horse. They say you can drag a horse TO water, but try dragging one through water. It's not easy.

Since I had missed my turn, I had to push it to the next entrance. I soon found out, that was at the deep end of the "Robbin's River". The spectators on the shore of the Robbins, were getting a real laugh out of me and a few other fools splashing around out in this world's biggest mud puddle. They should have charged admission for the entertainment.

"What an idiot" Someone felt compelled to share that snickering commentary with anyone who hadn't yet figured out that we who were knee deep in the flood, were not among Boeing best and brightest.

If I wasn't half submerged and being plummeted by the pour rain push my car, I would have still been soaked and standing in a puddle of my own sweat. This was the hardest I'd ever worked at Boeing, and I hadn't even made it into the parking lot yet.

But amid all the taunting crowds, was a hero waiting to help save me, named Tommy T, whom I barely knew.

Although he was now off work, just sticking around for the show, he took mercy on me. He knew, that I would never be able to push my amphibious horse up the ramp into the parking lot by myself. So Tommy, all warm and dry, took off his shoes, and put them in his car. Then he rolled up his pant legs, and joined me for the fun in the water.

With the extra oomph...we struggled, but were finally able to get my car onto the high ground of the parking lot. Tommy was just a small man, but it was just enough extra push to bring my submarine into the dry dock. Tom was small, but what a big heart he had!

Between gasps, trying to catch my breath, I thanked him profusely. And reached into my back pocket, to pull out my soggy wallet, to find some reward money.

"No thanks Eddy....just pass on the favor to someone else sometime" Tommy said, as I waved a couple dripping five dollar bills at him.

But for his valor, bravery, and kindness in the face of my stupidity, Tommy is high on my list of Boeing heroes. It's that kind of loyalty, brotherhood and grace, that is part of that Boeing "working together" spirit. I'll never forget Tommy's altruistic gesture on that bad day for me, for my car and for my attendance record.

Similarly, at the Thompson site, I once had a flat at quitting time. I'd meant to get around to it, but I guess I'd forgotten to fix my spare that had gone flat some months ago.

Left penniless from the last strike, and without AAA, what was I going to do at 11 o'clock at night, when I was just about the last man standing on the Boeing property?

I don't remember the exact details (blame it on the Keytone), but I remember John G, coming out of the building as I was scratching my head wondering how I was going to get home. I think he tried his own spare, but the bolt pattern was wrong. Like I say, I'm fuzzy on the specifics, he may have run down to the local store for some fix a flat for me. But I recall his determination to help me out of my fix.

"I've got a wheel like this one at home, in Bonny Lake. I could run home and get it and bring it back" I remember him offering.

Bonny Lake wasn't just down the block from the Boeing complex on East Marginal. It's about 35 miles each way. But John was willing to go that far to help out a friend, after a long grueling night working on the engine buildup line.

202

John was another fine example of the quality of character of the "Lazy B"s. Sometimes, Union brothers were brothers of the highest caliber. Somehow, he made sure I got safely on my way, before he went safely on his own way. Thanks again John!

My next hero, was also my nemesis. It was "Scotch". the same guy who made me pay over and over again for my McDonald's hamburgers. When I had moved from 2nd shift to 3rd at Renton, he had been a great encourager to me. But, that's not why he made my hero list.

When the well loved and respected supervisor, Frank T retired, Scotch was bucking for the management job. And I enthusiastically rooted for him to get it. He was smart, he knew the cranes well, and I thought he would be the perfect replacement for Frank. And his first big action as a manager, convinced me that my appraisal was right on target.

On the factory floors, real estate is precious. The production shops don't want to give an inch of their "property" away. Despite the fact that our line moves were taking place in the "S and I" jigs at the south end of the 4-82 building, our slings were stored far away, towards the middle of the building.

Someone suggested, that we ought to keep our slings at the "point of use". An excellent idea, but everyone knew that the shop would never surrender any space for this cause, in their already crowded, and cramped work area.

But Scotch, in an amazingly "ballsy" move, told us to land our slings right there on top of the S and I, and leave them there. He didn't ask, because surely the answer would be not just no, but "Hell NO". I was impressed by his brave, defiant move.

But first thing in the morning, it was sure to be a big issue as the manufacturing chiefs got together, and started their war dance. Even if we were allowed to smoke in the factory, it would take more than passing the peace pipe around, to steal this piece of land from the tribe.

How could he get away with this attempt at "eminent domain", for the good of the crane crew?

The ambitious, and intelligent Scotch, did so, by writing up a compelling and convincing "business case" for our slings being readily available. We could give our customer superior, and more timely service by keeping the slings at the point of use.

He documented the time savings and advantages, in a way that no deciding arbitrator could argue with. "This helps us, to help and serve you better" was the crux of his message. We prevailed, and the crane crew "took" the hill.

Over the years, Scotch and I had our differences. But I still tip my hat to his "Wild West" approach to taking over the townsfolk's homestead, for the overall good of Boeing. It was like the showdowns they used to do in the golden days at the "Lazy B" ranch. Yee Haw, Scotch!

The crane crew was full of heroes and legends. Of course there was Chuckie "M", who was kind of the heart of the crane crew. A good natured guy who would always bring in goodies to keep us all full and happy.

There was Bruce "W", a highly regarded long time veteran of cranes, who earned the utmost respect from all. He tried hard to make me into a 4-20 crane operator, but the challenge of molding me into a 4-20 guy, was too much, even for him.

Also from the 4-20 land of the giants was Bobby "N". Helpful, knowledgeable, and personable as an operator, he kept those virtues shinning brightly when he became a manager as well. Probably more than anyone else, Bobby was confident that he could teach me to master the 4-20 cranes. I never did, but it wasn't for a lack of Bobby trying his best.

And there was Roy "R", who kept us all entertained with his unique manner of telling his unique stories. Roy was always the first operator to arrive each morning, to boost the morale of the crew with laughter. Sadly, Roy only was able to enjoy a few months of retirement, before a heart attack took him away from us.

A couple of my own personal favorite heroes, were probably not as famous as some of the rest.

The two Lyles. Both Lyle "B" and Lyle "E" showed confidence in me in learning the 4-82 cranes, when people with more sense would have given up on me. Lyle "E" in particular, helped indoctrinate me into the bizarre world of Renton, as I had just left the comfortable Thompson Site plant. Being relatively new himself, he befriended me from day one, and took the extra time to tutor me.

Lyle "B" showed me endless patience, as I struggled through the impatience of some of my other trainers. Both Lyle's were tireless workers, who spent much time coming in early and staying late, as well as surrendering most of their weekends to keep Boeing flying high. They were truly Boeing "All Stars".

I never met Dean "M", who was probably the most famous of our Boeing crane operators. I was working at the Thompson Site when I heard the tragic news that his cab had run off the end of the rail, entrapping him, critically injured in his mangled crane as he bled out. His horrific accident caused the company to incorporate new safety features into our cranes, that may save lives in the future.

My last hero, was also named Dean. He wasn't a crane operator, but as a tooler we worked closely with him in our crane job. Like the Lyles, Dean "L", never knew how to say "no", to overtime. But, on straight time or OT, Dean was there to work. Always with a smile. Frequently all banged up.

Dean had come from the armpit of Boeing, the wing-line, as a lead. He was often injured as he tried to push himself and his crews to get the job done. As a tooler, he kept that strong work ethic alive, and was one of the most dependable workers I'd met in Renton.

That's why it was a mystery when he hadn't shown up for work for better than a week. One of his tooling coworkers, asked that the police do a welfare check on Dean. The cops found him dead at the top of his staircase. I think he was barely 50 years old. Dean probably worked himself to death. He will always be missed.

This is my short, non exclusive, "Hall of Fame" list. Anyone who worked at Boeing had their own colleagues who inspired them, and collectively were part of that intangible, Boeing Spirit. These employees influence moved far beyond their own tool boxes. But their associates and the company at large were better for their contributions.

Some of these were from the more civilized days of Boeing, from the late 80s onward. But I'm most fond of the untamed, wild Dodge City days of Boeing in the 70s....

22

NOT THAT DIFFERENT FROM THE 1800'S

"Harnesses? We don't need no stinkin' harnesses..."

It was kind of like the "Old West" back at the "old" Boeing saloon of the 1970s. The Generals were like the sheriffs, and the supervisors were like the deputies. When a superintendent would mosey through the shops, everyone scattered and hid. They were like the feared gunslingers.

Everybody was "Packing" in those times. . Some had paint guns, others shot cannons of sandblast hoses. The sound of rivet gun fire constantly echoed through the canyons of the factories.

The civil war would be relived a couple times each decade, as the "rebels" in the corporate offices would battle against the "Union". Until Tom Baker would give his Gettysburg address, and we would again become the United States of Boeing.

Without a net, Boeing workers would swing from girders, and dangle over the edges of high places to get their work done. Dangerous? Sure, but that came with the territory. Rarely did anyone die. But if they did, they would die with "their boots on". Probably NOT their steel toe boots though ...

The forklift guys, rode their horses pretty much "bareback". No heaters, no windows, not even roofs. Just a "roll bar" cage above them. Their rickety old steads, would sometimes travel across the bumpy trails, a bit skewed, so they even rode them, "side saddle".

The "wagon trains" were shuttles full of tub skids and dumpsters, miles long at Plant 2. They would stretch from the wastelands of reclamation, to the desserts of the hot tanks in the north property. They were so long, that before they even moved them, they would be at their destination.

No load was too big for their rigs. If their "jitney" was about to topple over, they'd just ask a few passerbys to climb on the back of their forklift to act as a "counterweight". Given enough people, a forklift, and a place to stand, they could lift the world.

"Steel toes and safety glasses are for sissies", the crusty old men would scoff. Sporting their eye patches, and balling their hands into three fingered fists as they limped away.

My Dad and the other Generals would roll up their sleeves and have their brawls in their offices once in a while.

Fists would pound on desks, and office supplies would fly around the room, like the chairs and bottles flew in the watering holes of old. After the walls shook with angry cuss words, on several occasions Dad threw his badge in his bosses face, before storming off in a cloud of dust.

Before he would fire up his car and drive off into the sunset however, his boss would come and get him, and they would hammer out their differences.

In the shops, sometimes fisticuffs would break out. If management or security caught wind of it, the fighters would hang. And never be seen again in these here parts. But mostly, they would keep these brawls to themselves. Wiping their bloody noses, and shaking hands as friends when it was over.

The women folk mostly stayed safely tucked away inside in the offices tending to paperwork. As the men would grit their teeth and twist iron into airplanes.

Of course, the guys would naturally leer at the pretty women too. It was an unwritten clause in the girl's job title, that they were there to keep morale up, and keep smiles on the faces of the fellas. It wasn't chauvinistic, it was just a different time back then. Most ladies considered being followed around by those eyes, a compliment. You're welcome, ladies.

They certainly didn't launch a lawsuit, or run to HR. That vicious animal hadn't evolved yet.

We solved our own problems, man to man. There were no skirts to go running underneath screaming, "Make them STOP!" "Human Relations" was just that. Humans relating to each other.

Ninety nine percent of the time, problems were just ironed out between parties on their own. Rarely did anyone elevate their issues to the boss. If they did, someone would probably be in trouble. I never went to the boss, or to HR once that monster had hatched. in all of my 37 years.

Boeing today is like a monastery compared to the Boeing where I became a man.

No smoking, no drinking, no dirty books, no dirty looks. No cussing, no fussing, no piling on the back of a forklift to let it lift many times it's own weight, like an ant.

Workers are suspended like puppets with fall protection lines, rather than the daring acrobats who used to walk tightropes in high beams with no nets to catch them.

Instead, just like Monks in Ivory snow coveralls, they make their pilgrimage each day to a sparkling clean factory. Carefully walking inside the paint striped walkway lines, afraid to step out of line.

Pacified by coffee and loud music, wearing more safety gear that weighs more than they do. Like trained dogs, jumping at the sound of the whistle, hoping the master will throw them a good sized bone. If they dared to "strike", they would soon be euthanized.

Rather than burly men wielding picket signs demanding that Boeing give up a piece of the pie, their power has been reduced to children pulling at the apron strings,

"Mommy? Can I have a cookie?"

"Not until you finish your IAW...."

Managers are invalid, unable to fire, manage, or decide much of anything without the validation, blessings and decrees of Human Relations.

HR stalks the grounds, like headhunters, thinly disguised in power suits, ready to extinguish any nonsense. And clear the smile off of any face who finds enjoyment in their vocations.

The slices get thinner and thinner, as competitiveness pounds the flesh of the employees lean, like a meat hammer. It's a bright, clean, orderly, dismal place to work.

Gone is the spirit. The eagerness to work like superheros when needed, and to party like animals when they could.

The torch has been passed. And although it still burns brightly, it is regarded with fear of being burned, rather than respected with pride. .

Gone is the filth and grit that used to waft in the air, and settle on the pavement. Slimy, vaporous spills are quickly eradicated, by a crack Haz Mat team in white astronaut suits. We used to step around them for weeks. Sometimes even gave names to the puddles.

It may be safer, more efficient, and structured, but Boeing is not half as much fun as it was in the "bad old days".

Bill Boeing would probably crush his cigarette, and smash his whiskey bottle, turning over in his grave.

Thinking, "What happened to the SPUNK?"

It's still a good place to work. You just need to enjoy yourself on the outside, and bring your own donuts, hats and thermoses to work. Consider yourself lucky to get a paycheck, and a pass to see the doctor when you get sick.

There were all kinds of hi-jinks that took place in the badlands of Boeing. But the one thing that wouldn't work in the wild, wild Boeing prairie town, was bad attendance. It was the surest, quickest way to get sent to "boot hill"

It didn't matter so much, what you did or didn't do once you were here. But you had better "be here" when you're supposed to be. Or you'd hang, by dang!

But when the gun smoke dissipated, and we all saddled up to go home, by gum, there were airplanes and missiles flying though the air.

It was how the skies were won.

23

THE SWEET, BY AND BYE...

By 2010 or so, all of the fences of the old wild west days at Boeing had been trampled down by a new breed of management.

All of the "dinosaurs" like my Dad, who would breathe fire, and scare you into compliance, had been replaced by calmer, gentler figureheads, who had no power of their own. But they're backed up by the full force and authority of the unquestionable mightiness of HR and Security.

Even the carefree, annual company barbecues where they once smiled their thanks, and said "Take your time...Have all that you want" were now closely regulated by managers.

Stamping your hands, and watching their watches. Portions were carefully measured and accounted for. No more plates to take home to share with your wife. And of course, we needed to "hurry up and eat", because, "We have planes to build if we're going to beat Airbus"

Something in the potato salad has gone bad.

Everyone knows, that across the pond, they're not counting the bones on the barbecue. Like their paychecks, it's all government subsided at Airbus. I get it. Here in the land of free enterprise, there's no extra sauce on those burgers. But, it's a bit of a "culture shock" for those of us who grew up in the "land of plenty". The times, they truly are "a changing".

Everyone wants the company to succeed. But as they have always done, the company will play that competition card, until the ink is completely worn off of it.

The threat of competition does have some legitimacy. But they trump it up for all it's worth, to put more in the company piggy bank, and less in the pockets of the workers. It's not a new game. It's been played since the dawn of industry.

The old timers know this. But the new kids coming in, are too naive to realize how the game is played. They believe everything that they are told by the company.

The company devalues their contributions. They threaten them into signing depreciating, 10 year, "No Strike" deals. They bribe them into drinking the poison, by waving cash bonuses under their noses. While they smile at them and tell them what "good friends" they are. The snakes themselves, have become the snake oil salesmen.

I'm not talking about the "shop supervisors". Most of them are just regular guys, who came from the same ranks that we did. And, if anyone has a right to be "scared", it's them. They have no "Union Security" to fall back on anymore.

If I sound a little bitter, I guess I am. Not just Boeing, but across industry, the workers did it to themselves. Solidarity and negotiations through leverage were never meant to bankrupt companies. Just to give the workers a "fair shake".

The unions needed acknowledge the business realities, of the companies (not the smoke that the companies blow up their behinds, but the real challenges they face). And make sure that the demands they demand, are consistent with the success of the company. But, not consistent with the "excess" that the company wants. The "bargain" has to make sense to both sides.

On the other hand, the company should realize the value of a "loyal, committed workforce", with an undying commitment to keeping the company "number one". That is not achieved or nurtured, by de-funding pension plans, and cannibalizing health plans. Especially, as you brag about your record profits, and skyrocketing stock prices.

I understand that international competition has muddied the waters. But I also understand it has become "vogue" in the corporate world, to laugh at the workers who build their goods, as they strip their compensation down to measly shadows of what it takes to support a middle class livelihood.

From the ivory towers, it's a fun game to play, I guess. But it's also fool-hearty to play such games with the ones that you want to help you to succeed. Take care of them, and they will do everything that they can, to take care of you.

But in their well conceived wisdom, Boeing started first by milking the well kept secrets and skills of the old timers into documented, "Work Processes". Then after brainwashing the "children" who had newly entered the workforce, they alienated the old timers.

Once we had to wait 25 years for the coveted "inside parking pass". It was a small token, but a meaningful reward for those who had stuck with the company for their working lifetimes. Then, they upped the requirement to 30, and later 35 years.

When I finally got mine, they had reconfigured the parking and sent EVERYONE outside of the inner gates at Renton. Making those treasured parking passes, worthless. And added hundreds of "handicapped" parking stalls inside.

I'm all for accommodations for the disabled. But on all shifts, most these handicapped stalls were left empty. Were they expecting a rash of injuries to happen, "any day now"? That was very unlikely, with all of the ridiculously strict "safety rules", some of which made it difficult to do our jobs at all.

Speaking of safety, in this same era, in a company sponsored, "crane egress" training class, where we were taught how to exit the crane cabs lowering ourselves down a rope line in case of an emergency, my friend Chucky was badly injured.

The pulley that was supposed to let him down easy, failed, and he came crashing down hard. Badly injuring his shoulder. Not only did he have to fight the pain and adapt to his new limited range of motion, he also had to battle the company for his rightful compensation.

And Brent, following our usual procedure for rigging the "Texas Tower" platform that workers stood on to install the stabilizers on the airplane, was surprised by the safety police telling him that the "rules had changed".

No one on our shift was aware of this new regulation. But instead of noting it, educating our crew, and solving the problem, they walked him out the gate.

Brent was a conscientious worker who always tried to do the right thing. He was a proud man, and this suspension really hurt his pride. It was also tough, not knowing what his fate was going to be. He hadn't knowingly done anything wrong. But in the new Boeing, they shoot first, and ask question later.

Brent spent his week off, fretting over the incident. He was eventually exonerated of any wrongdoing. And was reinstated with full pay for his suspension. But it was a demoralizing time, and a loss for both our crew, the company, and even for the integrity of the safety program's policies.

For no good reason, Boeing had taken what might have been a win/win learning experience, that made us all safer, and turned it into a lose/lose debacle, for everyone.

So, there I was, nearing age 60. A pretty good forklift driver, trapped by my own lust for money, in the body of a crane operator. Doing the best I could in my profession, but just barely squeaking by.

That was my own fault, not Boeing's. If I had stayed where I was, I might still be driving jitney, and getting paid for it today. As they say, the love of money is the root of all evil.

But I wasn't making a ton of money. Not only was I passing up the overtime that my colleagues were making, in an attempt to dodge working in that despised 4-20 building, I was also often sidelined at home with my debilitating sinus headaches.

I had "Family Leave" to cover my lost time. But Family Leave is unpaid hours. Akin to migraine headaches, these sinus problems would be so intense that I could hardly see straight. And to add frosting to my cake, my back went out walking up a staircase during my last year with the company.

As much as I loved driving forklifts, I'm pretty sure that my back issues started in the seat of my jitney, way back in the 1990s.

With a big crate on my forks, I was driving backwards, looking over my left shoulder, when my right wheel fell into a huge chuckhole on my blind side. My forklift dipped down and then lunged up as it hit the edge of the hole. It caused me to jump up out of my seat, and then come down harshly, while my back was twisted.

It gave me some discomfort at the time, but a few weeks later, it was like someone had hit me in the back with a two by four. I spent the next week mostly on my back. My only exercise was slinking out of bed, to crawl to the bathroom.

Since that time, it would flare up now and then, sometimes I would even need a cane or a walker. But that most recent back issue was different. My back would ache ruthlessly, fatiguing after spending any more than five or ten minutes on my feet.

Healing was slow, and incomplete. I couldn't work under the circumstances, and went on L and I for nearly two months. To this day, I still have problems with back fatigue and aching frequently. I guess I'm getting old.

The constant bending over and looking through your legs, goes with the job of being a crane operator. It has been well documented that the crane job does contribute to back injuries.

As a project for one of our work, "improvement teams", I researched and wrote up the particulars of the back strain caused by our posture, and possible solutions with specially engineered, "ergonomic" crane seats. I don't know if the company ever followed up on this, but if so, they may avoid or minimum future injuries such as mine.

Besides my back problems, my chronic headaches. and my general dissatisfaction with my chosen field, I was also suffering from some "mystery ailment" that was giving me general fatigue, odd pains, and general malaise. Added all together, it seemed like my days here were numbered.

But, I probably would have rode it out for at least a couple more years, to build my pension a little more. But as I've mentioned, Boeing had frozen the pension funds, and was no longer contributing to them.

The straw that broke the fat guy's back was when a combination of my mistake, and a malfunction in the cranes almost sent one of my crane partner's plummeting down 80 feet to the ground. ALMOST, thank God.

Our cranes had a "remote" function, that would allow us to control another bridge from our own cabs. Ken, a great guy and excellent operator was on a bridge, that I was supposed to move out of the way, once he had finished traveling to another bridge. I glanced over my shoulder and swore that I saw him, safely on that new bridge, he was traveling to.

So I returned to my control panel and hit the switch that would unlock the bridge that I needed to move. And then I sent the bridge on it's way.

There is an override built into the computerized controls that is not supposed to let me move that bridge, if there is another cab on it.

Ken's cab was on that bridge, and the override failed to block my commands.

As the bridge I attempted to move broke free, Ken's cab was straddled between the moving bridge and the stationary one that he was trying to travel to. If not for his quick wits, he might have come right off the rails and plunged to his death. Ken jammed his controls and raced across, just in the nick of time.

We had lost a crane operator named Dean back in 1999, in the 4-20 building when the "stop dogs" at the end of the rail failed to engage, and this could have easily been another disaster.

My fellow operators were sympathetic, continuing to remind me that "we all make mistakes" and "it wasn't your fault, it was a crane malfunction"

But what little confidence I had had been shaken. Tallying up all my physical problems, this troubling incident, and my alienation with all the changes that were transforming this company that I loved, into one I no longer knew...I figured it was time to go.

Even if I had decided to go back into the cabs, for my role in this "near miss", I was told I would have to "re-certify" in all the buildings, including the 4-20. Basically start all over again.

My compassionate crane partners cried bloody murder, as this was a new way of responding to an operator error, or incident. Boeing had never done this before when someone made an error.

Yet I kind of understood the companies response, given the gravity of the potential harm and damage this might have caused. Nevertheless, I appreciated the support and understanding of my crane brothers.

But I was done. Whether they tried to put a fork in me, or a forklift under me...Clearly, I was done.

I could have stuck around, perhaps even changed fields. But after so many years, the thrill was gone. I really wanted, and needed to retire.

Time to finally get that "sabbatical", that my Dad had denied me after High School. Set a new record for my longest "break-time" ever. Time to go on a long vacation. A PERMANANT vacation....

Since some time has passed, it all makes sense now. Everything happens for a reason.

I've pretty much reconciled with everybody and everything that happened. I learned much about myself, the world, and about life working at the Lazy B. I'll list some of the lessons, starting at the end, and going back to the beginning.

I learned to "know when to hold, know when to fold 'em", Thanks Boeing, and Kenny Rogers, for showing me when to hang it up.

I learned that I'm in control, not my bladder. Thank you cranes, for teaching me that urinary urgency can be suppressed for hours if need be, when you're stuck on a crane job.

I learned that company's are meant to make money, not make to people happy. Thanks Boeing, you're doing an exceptionally fine job at that these days.

I learned not to cross the boss, nor bite the hand that feeds you. Thanks Scotch, for making that abundantly clear to me. Who knows? If I'd been in your shoes, I might have done the same.

But if I had it to do all over again, NOBODY would have gotten a hamburger from me. And I would have spent more time happily at home in final assembly, rather than being the weak link in the 4-20.

I learned that not everybody is a straight shooter, and that we need to watch our backs at all times. Thanks "Tex" for that reminder.

I learned that when a boss wants to hold you down, sometimes you have to talk sense to his boss to rise above it. Thanks, Marshmallow. Although, you were probably right. I did make a better forklift driver than a crane operator.

I learned that "just in time" works great for inventory, not so much for attendance. Probably best, to leave an extra five minutes early for work.

And finally, I learned that there's nothing better for making a pesky "Lazy Bee" boss in a nice suit scram, than a blast of spray paint from a wayward airless paint gun. Thanks Dick!

It was fun, it was long, it was crazy, and it kept me off the streets. Overall, I'm immensely grateful for the time I spent working at Boeing.

I learned how to last for 37 years at the Lazy B. Now, I just need to learn how to last another 37 years at being retired.

EPILOUGE

We were a different breed, but Boeing people really cared. We were all proud of the roles we played, both big and small in the success of the company.

By and large, across the board, we met or exceeded the expectations that were set for us. Painters kept the place looking nice. Maintenance utility men were glad to lend a hand, and thrilled if they could learn something in the process. Forklift drivers got everything to where it needed to be, no matter how we had to do it.

Crane operators would find a way to achieve the impossible lifts, through the synergy of their skills and knowledge. Throughout the Boeing company, Yankee ingenuity thrived. And collectively, we were all determined to make Bill Boeing proud.

Sometimes the company's expectations for us were low, other times they were stellar. In my later years at the company, the bar seemed to be attached to helium balloons, raising ever higher,

And no matter how lofty the goals were, we always seemed to find a way to achieve them. In the midst of the company's drive to ask for more, for less...the resolve of their employees still kept the Boeing jets flying high.

We came from all walks of life. Every type of personality. And every skill and work ethic made up our workforce. Yet, once we were accepted into the "club", we would all work together to give wings to the company dreams.

Some came in just for the money and the benefits, but would soon be caught up in the enthusiasm of their colleagues. That, "We're number ONE" spirit, would soon rapture the souls of anyone on the crew, from the janitor to the CEO. And inspire them to strive to be their best. Working for Boeing, we were "Bad", in a very good way.

As our planes roared through the skies, each of us would gaze up with pride, knowing that we had helped give flight to our success. We may have joked about working at the "Lazy B", but we knew in the eyes of the world, we were all a part of the "Mighty B". And every bit as important as the pilot in making it airborne.

I think that when Boeing was our "hometown hero", even more-so than later, we were more than workers. We were teammates, on a winning team. In the big Superbowl of the skies, we all saluted our planes, like a flag. I would board a 737, and boast to the flight attendants that I had, as a crane operator, flown this bird before anyone else. I felt like a rock star.

A big part of our proud, heritage was our "brotherhood" and "sisterhood" as part of the Boeing family. Solidified by our union roots, and our caring for one another, we would protect and boost one another.

Sometimes that meant, concealing our injuries, so that our crew could enjoy the rewards of our impeccable safety record. Other times it would mean tutoring, or even covering for one of our colleagues who was struggling to bring their efforts up to snuff.

At times, it meant giving an ear and compassion to one of our Boeing siblings who was struggling with personal distractions, that were affecting their work performance. Other times it meant "leaning" on someone who had lost focus, and helping to "bring them back". But there was a rich value in the loyalty we granted one another.

As I neared retirement, I think the company had lost some of the awareness of the worth of the benefits of a loyal workforce. They surely understood and expected loyalty to the company, and rightfully so.

But the value of loyalty to one another and how that translates to an effective and motivated workforce, somehow evades the data that can be charted on graphs and tables. In my day, we worked with almost "blood oaths" to one another. We would never rat on a union brother or sister. But we would surely help them get on board when needed to accomplish our little part of the big picture.

When faced with challenges, as in a war...your best allies are those on the front lines, huddled together in the foxholes.

A battalion of those who would on command, be willing to stab one another in the back may charm the commanders. But they will lose the war. The camaraderie that we nurtured both on our jobs, and on the picket lines, is an intangible quality, that is only clearly evident when the battle becomes fierce.

Given contentment, a fair shake, and a healthy dose of morale, there is nothing that a Boeing crew couldn't, or wouldn't do for each other. Or for the company that they love and respect. Those attributes can't be cultivated in a field of takeaways, or in "every man for himself", under the company banner. They are only found in community and the shared commitment to the cause.

Boeing, give your employees the best you can, and they will give you the best they have. Give them some space to be humans, among the mechanized metrics of progress.

Be quick to praise their accomplishments. And slow to chastise their faults. Do all that you can to let them be happy, and watch them make you and your stockholders happy too.

Cherish, don't chastise their solidarity towards each other. Show your pride in who they are, and what they have to offer, and I assure you, they will make you proud.

As you face competition, don't mimic their success. Be bold enough to model success. With the treasured Boeing personality that made you who you have become over the years. Fertilize the feisty, determined, laugh together, fight together resolve, that put this little company alongside the river, on the maps of the world.

225

There has been a trend to devalue the human effort, as automation displaces them Remember, when machines take over building the planes, only machines will be able to afford to fly in them.

When I turned in my badge and retired, I looked around at my crane colleagues, who were starting out young as I once was. In a much different company than the one I started with in the 1970s.

A changing of the guard was taking place, as many of us "old timers" hung up our hardhats and orange gloves. Seeing the considerable talents and the zeal of these fresh young faces, I smiled. "The company is in GOOD hands"

Given the respect and accolades they deserve, I knew there was nothing the company could throw at them that they couldn't handle..

The "Snap On" swimsuit calendars and the drunken Christmas parties may be a thing of the past. But the excitement of being a part of the future of flight can be as alive now, as it has ever been.

The "Lazy B" has now become an oxymoron.. But if everyone plays their cards right, when these new guys become old and retire, they too will smile with pride reflecting back on the "Beautiful B", that they were a part of.

ABOUT THE AUTHOR

I spent 37 years floating between jobs and plants at the "Lazy B". Working in variety of positions, and meeting countless Boeing workers, I have seen the good, the bad and the ugly.

For most companies and professions, it would be hard to justify a memoir about "work" that would be engaging to the reader. But the "Lazy B" was different. If those factory walls could talk, what stories they could tell!

I tried to give those walls vocal chords in this book. It was hard to avoid a little political commentary as I contemplated the changes I've seen through the decades.

In reality, I have a hard enough time balancing my own checkbook. I have no expertise on how to run a successful airplane company. So please take my commentary with a dash of discernment.

Some may agree and other disagree with my analysis. But "The Lazy B" is strictly a look at things through my eyes. I hope you found it interesting, even if you saw an entirely different Boeing in your experiences.

Some of my bombastic comments were blunt and critical. But they weren't meant to insult anyone. They were just necessary to pen my honest account of the Boeing that I knew. Although you can no longer have a Margarita on Boeing premises, please take my opinions with a grain of salt.

From the bottom of my heart, I still feel that the Boeing company, and the Boeing people especially, are the best.

Thanks for Reading!
-Fast Eddy

OTHER BOOKS BY FAST EDDY

The Land of the Hazelnuts
A lighthearted memoir about growing up in the suburbs
of Seattle in the 1960s and 70s

Taming Hercules
Fast Eddy's first fictional book, about
raising a headstrong Alaskan Malamute
who dreams to dominate his world, in
his vivid dreams.

Good Times on the High Seas
A book about the joys of cruising on a
luxury Ocean Liner. Great tips on how
to have more fun, and save money
on the vacation of your dreams.

All are available on Amazon.com

Made in the USA
Las Vegas, NV
18 May 2023

72240868R00131